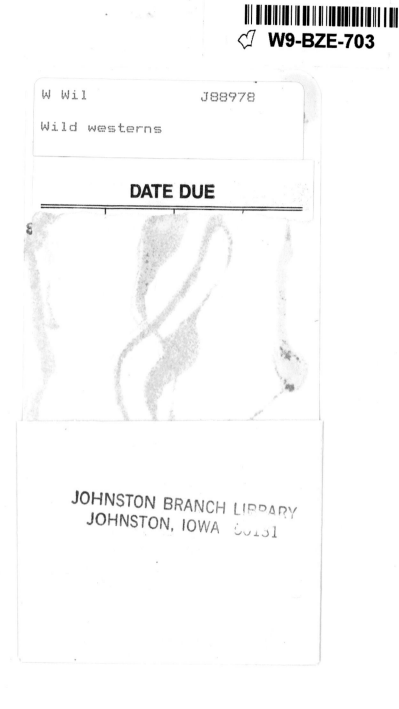

Wild Westerns

WILD WESTERNS

Stories from the Grand Old Pulps

Edited by Bill Pronzini

Walker and Company WITHDRAWN
New York

First published in the United States of America in 1986 by the Walker Publishing Company, Inc.

Published simultaneously in Canada by John Wiley & Sons Canada, Limited, Rexdale, Ontario

Library of Congress Cataloging-in-Publication Data

Wild westerns.
    1. Western stories.   2. American fiction—20th century.   I. Pronzini, Bill.
PS648.W4W55   1986   813'.0874'08   86-13220
ISBN 0-8027-4066-9

Printed in the United States of America

10 9 8 7 6 5 4 3 2 1

CONTENTS

ACKNOWLEDGMENTS

"The Laughter of Slim Malone" by Max Brand. Copyright © 1919 by Frank A. Munsey Company; copyright renewed © 1947 by Popular Publications, Inc. Reprinted by permission of Brandt & Brandt Literary Agents Inc.

"Swindle at Piute Sink" by Luke Short. Copyright © 1939 by Street & Smith Publications, Inc. First published in *Western Story Magazine*. Reprinted by permission of H. N. Swanson, Inc., agents for the estate of Frederick W. Glidden (Luke Short).

"Lawyer Two-Fist" by Wayne D. Overholser. Copyright © 1939 by Street & Smith Publications, Inc. First published in *Western Story Magazine*. Reprinted by permission of the author.

"Enough Gold" by W. Ryerson Johnson. Copyright © 1939 by Street & Smith Publications, Inc. First published in *Western Story Magazine*. Reprinted by permission of the author.

"I.O.U.—One Bullet" by Dan Cushman. Copyright © 1946 by Real Adventures Publishing Co., Inc. First published in *Lariat Story Magazine*. Reprinted by permission of Scott Meredith Literary Agency, 845 Third Avenue, New York, N.Y. 10022.

"Vigilante" by H. A. DeRosso. Copyright © 1948 by Popular Publications, Inc. First published in *New Western* under the title "Swing Your Pardner High!" Reprinted by permission of Scott Meredith Literary Agency, 845 Third Avenue, New York, N.Y. 10022.

"A Wollopin' Good Chew" by Thomas Thompson. Copyright © 1948 by Popular Publications, Inc. First published in *New Western* under the title "Follow the Signpost to Hell." Reprinted by permission of the author.

"Chivaree" by Frank Bonham. Copyright © 1951 by Popular Publications, Inc. First published in *Star Western* under the title "Lovely Little Liar." Reprinted by permission of the author.

INTRODUCTION

BETWEEN 1920 and 1950, pulp magazines ruled the popular fiction roost in the United States (and, to some extent, in Canada and England as well). Seven by ten inches in size, printed on untrimmed woodpulp paper, the pulps had gaudy enameled covers that depicted scenes of high melodrama. The stories they contained were just as gaudy and melodramatic as their artwork. They were the successors to the dime novels and story weeklies of the nineteenth century, mass-produced to provide cheap reading thrills for imaginative young adults and the so-called "common man," selling for a nickel or a dime in their early years and a quarter in their final ones. At the height of their popularity, in the midthirties, there were more than 200 different titles on the market—titles featuring stories of mystery, detection, adventure, war on land and sea and in the air, life in the Old West, modern-day romance, science fiction, fantasy, and sometimes sadistic horror.

Far and away the most popular pulps were Westerns. Such titles as *Western Story, Wild West Weekly, Ranch Romances, Texas Rangers,* and *Dime Western* perenially outsold those in all other categories throughout most of the pulp era. This is hardly surprising when you consider that the Western story is a uniquely American art form, and that as a result Americans have not only embraced fictional chronicles of the great westward expansion, but elevated them to the lofty status of myth. During this century the Western has been a symbol of all that America stands for: freedom, justice, self-reliance, the pioneer spirit. And in the Depression thirties and the war-torn forties, Americans *needed* that myth, that spirit to sustain them. The Western pulps, then, were more than just cheap entertainment, more than just an escape into the past; they were a hope for the future.

The first Western pulp was established by Street & Smith,

the dime-novel kings. In 1919 S&S revamped one of their dime-novel periodicals, *New Buffalo Bill Weekly,* into the pulp format and retitled the new biweekly *Western Story Magazine.* (At that time pulp magazines had been around for nearly twenty years. Frank A. Munsey had restructured *Argosy* into a pulp in the mid-1890's, and soon afterward brought out numerous other pulp titles, among them *All-Story Weekly, Popular Magazine,* and *The Railroad Man's Magazine.*) The circulation of *Western Story,* which sold for ten cents, burgeoned in the twenties, when Street & Smith made it into a weekly, and it remained one of the two or three top-selling titles throughout its three decades of life.

The success of *Western Story* inspired imitations and variations, of course. Doubleday brought out *West* and *Frontier Stories,* which would also prove to be long-running titles; William Clayton started *Cowboy Stories, Ace-High Western, Ranch Romances,* and *Western Adventures;* Fiction House produced *Lariat* and *North-West Stories* (the latter title proclaiming itself "the world's only all Western and Northern story magazine," and modestly announcing that what it published were "vigorous, tingling epics of the great *Snow* FRONTIER and the IMMORTAL WEST!"); and Street & Smith added *Far West, Wild West Weekly,* and *Pete Rice Magazine* to its stable. (Pistol Pete Rice, a rough-and-tumble Arizona sheriff with a coterie of deputies, was the first Western pulp hero to have his own magazine.) In the 1930s Ned Pines and his editorial director, Leo Margulies, started the Thrilling Group, which included such titles as *Thrilling Western, Popular Western, Texas Rangers,* and two Pete Rice rivals, *Masked Rider* and *Range Riders.* Harry Steeger's Popular Publications, eventually the largest and most active of the pulp chain publishers, also jumped on the bandwagon with *Dime Western, .44 Western, New Western, Star Western,* and *Big-Book Western.* And there were numerous other titles produced by independent and small-chain outfits, some of which flourished for a while but most of which were short-lived; among these were *Ace West-*

ern, Double-Action Western, Nickel Western, and *Mammoth West-ern.*

The paper shortage of World War II killed off a large number of titles. Others were purchased by the healthier chain publishers such as Popular and Thrilling and thus underwent changes in editorial policy. A few new titles were introduced during and after the war, and into the early fifties, including two named after Western pulp giants: *Max Brand's Western Magazine* and *Walt Coburn's Western Magazine.* But the handwriting was already on the wall: the pulps were doomed. The advent of war may have ended the Depression in this country, but it also began the decline and fall of the pulp kingdom; and in the war's aftermath, things began to change rapidly and radically everywhere. The publishing industry was especially vulnerable. Television and paperback books were the coming forms of cheap entertainment for the masses; there was little room for the pulps in the new and changing society.

Most titles were extinct by 1950. A few hardy ones, most of them Westerns—*Dime Western, Thrilling Western, Fifteen West-ern Tales, .44 Western, Real Western Stories, Texas Rangers*—hung on a few years longer. And *Ranch Romances,* amazingly enough, lasted until 1970 (although it was a mere shadow of itself at the end, publishing reprints almost exclusively), thus earning the distinction of being the longest-surviving pulp title.

The pulps may be long dead, but they are not forgotten. Not only did they provide entertainment for the masses; they provided a training ground for scores of writers who eventually went on to bigger and better literary endeavors. Stephen Crane, Jack London, Theodore Dreiser, Sinclair Lewis, Tennessee Williams, Horace McCoy, William E. Barrett, Paul Gallico, Dashiell Hammett, Raymond Chandler, Isaac Asimov, Ray Bradbury, Edgar Rice Burroughs, John D. MacDonald, Cornell Woolrich, Evan Hunter, Erle Stanley Gardner, and Rex Stout, among others, wrote for the pulp-paper market. And in the Western field, so did Zane Grey, Max Brand, Louis L'Amour, John Jakes, Elmore Leonard, Luke Short, William MacLeod Raine, Clarence E. Mulford, Ernest Haycox, Fred Gipson, Wayne D. Overholser, Elmer Kelton, Dan Cushman, Thomas Thompson, Lewis B. Patten, Les Savage, Jr., and Frank Bonham, to name just a few.

Much pulp fiction was of poor quality, to be sure; the stories were hastily written—many by hacks and amateurs in order to satisfy the annual demand for millions upon millions of words during the boom years—and the bulk of them should be allowed to crumble along with the woodpulp paper on which they were printed. But the best stories written by the best writers should not be lost to contemporary readers. This anthology offers just a small sampling of those worthy of reprinting.

Return with us now to those thrilling days of yesteryear (as the announcer used to say at the beginning of "The Lone Ranger"), when men were men and the West was still wild; when action and excitement were the bywords, and there were far more heroes than there were villains . . . the days when the pulps were king, and the king of the pulps was the Wild Western.

—Bill Pronzini

San Francisco, California
December, 1985

THE LAUGHTER OF SLIM MALONE

Max Brand

MAX Brand (Frederick Faust, 1892–1944) was the undisputed king of the Western pulps. Beginning with The Untamed *in 1918, and spanning slightly more than two decades, he published over 300 book-length Western serials and hundreds of shorter works, as well as hundreds more adventure, mystery, historical romance, medical (the Dr. Kildare series), and science fiction pulp novels and stories. He used eighteen other pseudonyms, among them George Owen Baxter, Evan Evans, David Manning, and George Challis. In the twenties and thirties he wrote entire issues of* Western Story Magazine, *often having two or three serials running concurrently. He also contributed numerous stories to such "slick" magazines as* Country Gentleman, Cosmopolitan, Good Housekeeping, *and* The Saturday Evening Post, *and somehow found time to pursue his first love, the writing of traditional poetry. All in all during a career that lasted some thirty years (and was cut tragically short by an enemy bullet while he was serving in Italy as a war correspondent during World War II), he produced the truly staggering aggregate of 17,000,000 words, making him the most prolific writer of this century and one of the most prolific of all time.*

"The Laughter of Slim Malone" is one of his earliest Western stories, having first appeared in All-Story Weekly *in 1919. Like most of his Old West tales, it relies as much on character and incident as it does on action, and contains, as one critic has written, that "leap of Faustian imagination . . . that urges the story beyond the established borders of the Western and into a vaguer territory of fantasy and universal myth."*

1

Time has little to do with reputation in the Far West, and accordingly the name of Slim Malone grew old in the region of Appleton, and yet the owner of the name was still young.

Appleton was somewhat of a misnomer, for the region had never known anything save imported apples or any other sort of fruit since the time of its birth into the history of whiskey and revolvers. But a misguided pioneer in the old days had raised a few scrubby trees and had named the town forever. The dreams of the early agriculturalists had died long ago, but the name remained to pique the curiosity of travelers and furnish jokes for inhabitants.

In the old days, when Appleton was a name rather than a fact, the hilarity had been as absent as the men; but after gold was discovered in the three gorges which led from the settlement into the heart of the mountains, the little town became a rendezvous of a thousand adventurers. The stages to and from the railroad thirty miles away, were crowded with men eager to face the hardships of the climate and the great adventure of the gold fields.

It was then that Slim Malone appeared. It was said that he had first come upon the scene as the owner of the Red River strike, which was finally owned by Sandy Gleason. It was further rumored that Sandy had beaten Slim Malone out of the claim by a very shady deal at cards; but Sandy refused to discuss the matter, and Slim Malone was rarely within vocal range, so the matter had never been sifted. Sandy was rarely more vocal than a grunt, and when Slim Malone appeared, people had generally other things to think about than questions concerning his past.

A certain percentage of lawlessness is taken for granted in a mining town. People are too busy with their own concerns to pay attention to their neighbors, but when three stages in succession, passing from Appleton to Concord, the nearest railroad station, were robbed by a rider on a white horse, the community awoke and waxed wrath. The loss was too much in common to be passed over.

The first effort was an impromptu organization of half a

dozen angered miners who rode into the Weston Hills. They found fresh hoofprints after an hour of riding, and went on greatly encouraged, with the pistols loosened in their holsters. After some hours of hard travel they came upon a white horse in the midst of a hollow, and then spread into a circle and approached cautiously. But not cautiously enough. While they were still far from the white horse the bandit opened fire upon them from the shelter of a circle of rocks. They rode into town the next day with three of their number badly hurt and the other three marked for life. That started the war.

As the months passed posse after posse left Appleton and started to scour the Weston Hills for the marauder. The luckiest of the expeditions came back telling tales of a sudden fusillade from an unexpected covert, and then a swift white horse scouring into the distance. The majority came back with no tales at all save of silent mountains and the grim cactus of the desert.

In the meantime the stages from Appleton to Concord were held up with a monotonous regularity by a rider of a fleet white horse.

Then the new mayor came to Appleton. He owned three claims on Askwarthy Gulch, and he ran on the double platform of no license for the Appleton saloons and the end of Slim Malone. His name was Orval Kendricks but that didn't count. What mattered was his red hair and the statements of his platform. Slim Malone celebrated the new reign by holding up two stages within the first five days.

But the new mayor lived up to the color of his hair, and proved worthy of his platform. He held a meeting of every able-bodied citizen in town three days after his inauguration, and in his speech the men noted with relief that he forgot to mention the saloons, and that he concentrated his attention on Slim Malone.

After a carefully prepared peroration, he built up to his climax by the proposal that the community import "Lefty" Cornwall, at a salary of five hundred dollars a month and five thousand bonus, to act as deputy sheriff until the apprehension of Slim Malone. Then the crowd applauded for they were equal to any measures for Slim Malone's suppression, even if it meant the importation of Lefty Cornwall.

The fame of Lefty had begun in Texas when he mortally wounded one greaser and crippled two others in a saloon fight. Since then it had increased and spread until he was a household word even farther north than Appleton. He came from that sunburned southland where a man's prowess was gaged by his speed and dexterity with his "irons," and even on that northern plateau of Appleton men knew that to cross Lefty Cornwall was death or murderous mutilation.

Appleton decreed the day of the arrival of the new sheriff a festival occasion. The farmers from the adjoining tableland drove into town, the miners from the three valleys rode down. And when the stage arrived from Concord the incipient sheriff dismounted in the midst of a huge crowd, and cheers which shook the signboard of Sandy Orton's saloon.

Now the mayor of Appleton had declared deathless war against the saloons in his platform, but since his election he had been strangely silent upon the liquor question. He was as canny as his red hair suggested, and he had a truly Scotch insight into the crucial moments of life. He perceived the arrival of Lefty Cornwall to be such a moment, and he perceived at the same time the correct way of meeting that crisis.

It was with surprise no less than pleasure that the throng heard the lusty voice of their chief official inviting them to Sandy Orton's saloon, and where they were in doubt, his beckoning arm put them right. They filled the saloon from bar to door, and those who could not enter thronged at the entrances with gaping mouths.

The sheriff was equal to the occasion. He mounted the bar much as a plainsman mounts a horse, and standing in full view of his fellow citizens, he invited Lefty Cornwall to join him in his prominent position. Nowise loath, Lefty swung the bar in the most approved fashion, and stood, locked arm in arm with the dignified official of Appleton. In the meantime the bartenders, thrilled equally with surprise and pleasure, passed out the drinks to the crowded room. It was apparently a moment big in portent to Appleton, and not a heart there but pulsed big with pride in their mayor.

"Fellow citizens," began the mayor, raising a large freckled hand for silence.

A hush fell upon the assemblage.

"Boys," began Orval Kendricks again, "this here is a solemn occasion. I feel called upon to summon the manhood of this here town to listen to my words, and I reckon that most of the manhood of the town is within hearin.' "

A chorus of assent followed.

"I don't need any Daniel Webster to tell you men that this here town is hard hit," continued Mayor Kendricks. "It don't need no Henry Clay to tell you that these diggin's are about to bust up unless we have the right sort of a strong-arm man in town. We've been sufferin' patiently from the aggressions of a red-handed desperado who I don't need to mention, because his name just naturally burns my tongue."

"Slim Malone!" cried a dozen voices. "We're followin' you, Chief!"

The mayor thrust his hand into his breast and extended the other arm in imitation of a popular woodcut of Patrick Henry.

"There may be some of you guys," cried the mayor, rising to the emotion of the moment, "there may be some of you guys who don't know the man I mean, but I reckon that a tolerable pile of of Appleton's best citizens spend a large part of their time cursing Slim Malone."

"We ain't through damning him yet," yelled a voice, and the crowd voiced their assent, half in growls and half in laughter.

"He has tricked our posse as an honest man would be ashamed to do," went on the mayor, warming to his oration, "and he has shot our citizens, and he has swiped our gold! I'm askin' you as man to man, can a self-respectin' community stand for this? It can't. What's the answer that Appleton makes to this desperado?"

He paused and frowned the audience into a state of suspense.

"There is only one answer to this gunfighter, and that answer stands at my right hand," bellowed the mayor, when he judged that the silence had sunk into his hearers sufficiently. "The name of the answer is Lefty Cornwall!"

The following burst of applause brought a momentary blush into even Lefty's cheek. At the reiterated demands for a speech he hitched at his revolver in its skeleton holster, removed his sombrero, and mopped his forehead with a ponderous hand. When it became evident that the hero was about to break into utterance the crowd became silent.

"Fellows," began the gunfighter, "makin' speeches ain't much in my line."

"Makin' dead men is more your game," broke in the wit of the assemblage.

The universal hiss attested that the crowd was anxious to hear the Texan gunman out.

"But if you are goin' to do me the honor of makin' me sheriff of this here county and this here city of Appleton," he continued, letting his eye rove down Appleton's one street, "I'm here to state that law and order is goin' to be maintained here at all costs. Right here I got to state that the only costs I'm referrin' to is the price of the powder and lead for this here cannon of mine."

The crowd broke in upon the speech with noisy appreciation, and many cries of "That's the stuff, old boy!"

"I been hearin' a tolerable pile about one Slim Malone," went on the new sheriff.

"So have we," broke in the irrepressible wit of the assemblage, only to be choked into silence by more serious-minded neighbors.

"Sure," agreed the sheriff. "I reckon you've heard a lot too much about him. But I'm here to state that all this talk about

Slim Malone has got to stop, and has got to stop sudden. I'm here to stop it."

He hitched his holster a little forward again as he spoke and a deep silence fell upon the crowd.

"Fellow citizens," he continued, spitting liberally over the side of the bar, "whatever gunplay is carried on around here in the future is to be done strictly by me, and all you men can consider yourselves under warning to leave your shootin' irons at home, unless you want to use them to dig premature graves."

This advice was received with an ironical chuckle of appreciation from the crowd.

"As for Slim Malone," he went on, "I'm goin' out into the Weston Hills to get him single-handed. I don't want no posse. I'll get him single-handed or bust, you can lay to that, and if I come back to this town without Slim Malone, alive or dead, you can say that Malone has the Indian sign on me."

Having finished all that he had to say, Lefty felt about in his mind to find a graceful manner of closing his exordium, when the mayor came to his assistance. He recognized that nervous clearing of the throat and wandering of the eyes out of his own first political experiences. Now, he raised his glass of colored alcohol and water, which in Appleton rejoiced in the name of Bourbon.

"Boys," he shouted, "there ain't no better way of showin' our appreciation of our new sheriff than by turnin' bottoms up. Let's go!"

The next thing was to find a proper mount. This proved a more difficult task. The sheriff knew horses from nose to hoof, and he was hard to please. At last he selected a tall roan with a wicked eye and flat shoulders which promised speed. These preparations made, he swung to the saddle, waved his hand to the crowd, and galloped out of town.

It was complete night before he reached the upper end of Eagle Head Canyon, and he was weary from the stumbling gait of his horse over the rocks.

Lefty was a very brave man, but like almost all of the physically courageous, he dreaded derision more than actual pain. Yet, in spite of this he finally decided that it was better to go back to the town and face the smiles than to remain through the cold night in these dread silences. As it was he felt that it was no use to hunt further, and he started back down the canyon. He had not gone far when his horse stumbled and commenced to limp.

Lefty got off with a curse and felt of the forehoofs. The difficulty proved to be a sharp, three-cornered rock which had been picked up under the shoe of the left forefoot. He was bending over to pry this loose between his fingers when he caught the glint of a light.

In his excitement he sprang upright and stared. At once the light disappeared. Lefty began to feel ghostly. His senses had never played him such tricks before.

He leaned over and commenced work on the stone again, but as he did so his eye caught the same glint of light. There was no possible mistake about it this time. He remained bent over and stared at it until he was certain that he saw a yellow spot of light, a long, thin ray which pointed out to him like a finger through the shadows.

But this time he took the bearings of the light carefully, and when he stood up he was able to locate it again.

He threw the reins over his horse's head and commenced to stalk the light carefully. Sometimes as he slipped and stumbled over the rocks he lost sight of it altogether, only to have it reappear when he had almost given up hopes of finding it again. And so he came upon the cave.

The light shone through a little chink between two tall boulders, and as Lefty pressed his eye to the aperture, holding his breath as he did so, he saw a long dugout, perhaps a dozen paces from end to end, and some five paces wide. Behind a partition at one end he heard the stamping of a horse, and as Lefty gazed, a magnificent white head rose behind the partition and looked fairly at him.

At first he saw no other occupant of the place, but by moving his eye to one side of the aperture he managed to get a glimpse of the bandit himself. There was no question about his identity. From the descriptions which he had heard while in Appleton, he knew him at once, the expressionless gray eyes, and the thin, refined face.

He sat tilted back in a heavy chair smoking a pipe and reading, and Lefty saw that he sat facing a blanket at the far end of the room. Evidently this was the entrance. So far as Lefty could see the bandit was unarmed, his two long guns lying on the table half a dozen paces away.

Very softly he crept along the side of the boulder, and finally came to an aperture, as he had expected. It was just wide enough for a man to press through, and from the chisel marks at his sides it had evidently been artificially widened from time to time. At the end of the narrow passage hung the blanket.

If Lefty had proceeded cautiously up to this point, his caution now became almost animal-like. Behind that blanket he had no idea what was happening. Perhaps the bandit had heard a noise long before, and was now crouched against the wall in another part of the place, ready to open fire at the first stir of the blanket. Perhaps he had stolen out of the cave by another entrance and was now hunting the hunter. The thought sent a chill down Lefty's back and he turned his head quickly. Then he resumed his slow progress. At the very edge of the blanket he paused for a long and deathly minute.

He swung the blanket aside and crouched in the entrance with his gun leveled. The little round sight framed the face of Slim Malone, who still sat reading quietly.

"Hands up," Lefty said softly.

Even then, with his bead on his man, he did not feel entirely sure of himself.

The meaningless gray eyes raised calmly from the book. It seemed to Lefty that a yellow glint came into them for a moment like the light that comes into an animal's eyes when it is angered, but the next moment it was gone, and he could not be sure that it had come there at all. The rest of the face was perfectly calm. Malone lowered the book slowly and then raised his hands above his head.

"Ah, Sheriff," he said quietly, "I see that you have arrived at last."

He felt strangely relieved after hearing his quarry speak. He stepped through the entrance and straightened up, still with the revolver leveled.

"In order to remove any strain you may be under," went on Slim Malone, "I'll assure you that I am quite unarmed. My guns are both lying on the table there. In order that you may make sure, I shall stand up, with my hands over my head, and turn around slowly. You can examine me to your own satisfaction."

He did as he had said, and Lefty's practiced eyes saw that there was not the suspicion of a lump under the clothes.

"Now," said Slim Malone, as he faced his captor again, and his smile was strangely winning. "I hope that I may lower my arms and we can commence our little party."

"Your end of this here party is all over, my beauty," said Lefty grimly, "except that the boys at Appleton may give you a little impromptu reception when we hit town."

"So I understand," smiled Slim Malone. "I have no doubt they will be glad to see me."

"Ain't no doubt in the world," grinned Lefty. warming to the perfect calm of this man. "Between you an' me, pal, I'm sorry to have to turn this little trick; but—"

Malone waved a careless and reassuring hand.

"Business is business, my dear fellow," he said.

"That bein' the case," said Lefty, "I'll have to ask you to turn around and put your hands behind your back while I put these here bracelets on. I don't want to discourage you any, but while I'm doin' it this here gun will be in my hand and pointin' at your back."

"Naturally," nodded Malone. "Quite right, of course; but before we start on our little jaunt back to the camp won't you have a drink with me? I have some really rare old stuff here."

Lefty grinned appreciatively.

"It's a good move, pal," he said, shaking his head with admiration, "an' I know that you're hard put to it or you wouldn't try such an old dodge on me. It's a good move, but down in Texas the booze stunt is so old that they've almost forgotten it—but not quite!"

"Ah," said Malone, with a little sigh of regret, "then I suppose we shall have to ride out in the night without a nip. Gets mighty chilly here before morning, you know."

But this fact had gradually dawned on Lefty during his ride up the valley, and as he looked forward to the journey back he shivered with unpleasant anticipation.

"I suppose the booze is the real thing?" he inquired casually.

"There are little bubbles under the glass," said Slim Malone with subtle emotion.

Lefty Cornwall sighed deeply. The taste of the Appleton bar whisky still burned his mouth. After all this fellow was a man. He might be a criminal, but Lefty's own past was not free from shady episodes. Furthermore, he was about to make five thousand dollars on presenting him to the good people of Appleton.

"If you sure want a drink before we start, go ahead," said Lefty.

"The bottle and a glass is over there in that little dugout on the wall," pointed Malone.

In the little open hutch on the wall the sheriff perceived a tall bottle which shimmered pleasantly in the torchlight.

"Go ahead," said the sheriff, "I reckon you know I'm watchin' all the time."

"Surely," said Malone pleasantly. "I know you're on your job all the time."

He walked over to the hutch and picked up the bottle and

the glass. He paused with the bottle tucked away under his arm.

"Queer thing," pondered Malone, "the same pack that held this bottle of whiskey held this also."

Lefty tightened his grip on the gun as Malone reached deeper into the hutch, but he straightened again and appeared carrying a large concert banjo.

"That fellow had taste," he continued, crossing the room and laying the banjo carelessly on the chair. "Just run your eyes over that banjo."

"Some banjo, all right," said the sheriff, "but hurry up with your drink, Malone. We've got to be on our way."

Malone uncorked the bottle and held it under his nose.

"The old aroma, all right," he pronounced. "You won't join me?"

Now the heart of the sheriff was a human heart, but his will was adamant.

"Not me, Malone," he answered. "I've been in the game too long. Can't drink on this sort of a job."

"Guess you're right," murmured Malone, letting the amber stream trickle slowly into the glass, "but it's too bad."

He raised the glass to his lips and swallowed half of the contents slowly.

"It looks like the real thing," the sheriff said judicially.

"It is," pronounced Malone with decision.

The sheriff shuddered with sympathy.

"I reckon," he said hesitatingly, "that you might pour me just a drop."

It seemed to him that as he spoke the yellow glint came into the eyes of Malone again, but a moment later it was gone, and he decided that the change had been merely a shadow from the wavering torchlight. He took the glass which Malone extended to him under the cover of the pointed gun and raised it slowly to his lips.

"Just stand a bit further back while I drink, pal," he said.

Malone obeyed, and the sheriff tilted the glass. It was, as

Malone had said, "the real old aroma," and the sheriff drew a deep breath.

"I reckon it ain't quite as old as you say," said the sheriff, feeling his way cautiously. "I reckon it ain't more than fifteen years old at the outside."

Malone paused, with the bottle suspended over the glass to consider.

"I thought that myself when I first drank," he nodded, "but that was before I got used to it."

The sheriff was inclined to agree. He also felt sure that one more drink would quite banish from his memory the taste of that one drink in Appleton. Moreover, the danger, if there was any, was slight, for Malone was taking drink for drink with him, and larger drinks at that. It was a sort of subtle challenge to the manhood of the sheriff, and he was as proud of his capacity for whisky as of his speed with a gun.

It was perhaps half an hour later that the sheriff indicated the banjo with a careless wave of the pistol.

"Play any?" he inquired, "or do you keep it around as sort of an ornament?"

"Both," smiled Malone. "It makes the place more home-like, you know, and then I sing once in a while, but not often."

"I'm a pretty good judge," stated the sheriff. "Blaze away, and I'll see you ain't interrupted. Been a long time since I had the pleasure."

He was, as he said, a fairly good judge, and he was delighted with the rich baritone which rang through the cave. After a time, as the whisky and the music melted into his mood, he began to call for old favorites, darky ballads, and last of all, for the sentimental ditties which have always charmed the heart of the rough men of the West.

As he sang, the bandit commenced, naturally, to walk back and forth through the cave, and the sheriff sat back in the chair and with half-closed eyes waved the revolver back and forth in time. He failed to note that as Malone walked up and down each time he made a longer trip, until at last he was pacing and turning close to the table on which lay the revolvers side by side. He did not note it, or if he did his mind was too thrilled with the tender airs and the tenderer liquor to register the fact clearly.

The music stopped. Malone had stooped over the table with the speed of a bird picking up a grain of wheat, and with the same movement he whirled and fired. The gun spun from the hand of the sheriff and he stood staring into the eyes which now beyond all doubt flared with a yellow.

"Now put your hands behind your back after you've thrown those bracelets to me," said Malone. "I naturally hate to break up this party, but I think you've had about enough whisky to keep you warm on the ride back, Lefty, my boy."

There was an insane desire on the sheriff's part to leap upon Malone barehanded, but he had seen too many fighting men in action before. He knew the meaning of those eyes.

"It's your game, Slim," he said, with as little bitterness as possible.

Appleton woke early the next morning. Someone shouted and then fired a pistol. The populace gathered at windows and doors, rubbing sleepy eyes which a moment later shone wide awake, and yawns turned into yells of laughter, for down the middle of Appleton's one street came the sheriff. He was sitting the roan horse, with his feet tied below the girth, and his hands tied behind his back. And even the weary roan seemed to feel in his drooping head the defeat of his rider.

Upon the back of the sheriff was a large piece of cardboard, upon which was printed in large letters the following:

I'M SENDING THIS BACK WITH MY SIGNATURE IN TOKEN OF A PLEASANT EVENING IN MY HOME IN EAGLE HEAD CANYON. I'M SORRY TO ANNOUNCE THAT I'M MOVED.

SLIM MALONE.

HOPALONG SITS IN

Clarence E. Mulford

HOPALONG Cassidy has become a legendary name in the annals of Western romance. But there is a certain schizophrenic nature to Hoppy's character: he is actually two different heroes, one fictional and the other cinematic. As created by Clarence E. Mulford in Bar-20 days *(1907), he is a tough, ornery, vice-prone cowboy who works on a Texas ranch called the Bar-20 and carouses with such fellow waddies as Buck Peters, Johnny Nelson, and Red Connors. As portrayed by William Boyd in no less than sixty-six B films between 1935 and 1948, he is a squeaky clean, congenial doer-of-good-deeds who never shoots first and prefers to use his brain instead of his brawn. It was Boyd, who purchased all film rights to the series in the mid-thirties, who changed Hoppy's image—some might say for the better, others might not. The Mulford stories about Cassidy are rousing adventures, with some of the best action sequences in early Western fiction; the Boyd films are morality plays with simplistic detective-story plots and plenty of broad humor, much of it provided by the likes of Gabby Hayes ("You're durn tootin', Hoppy"). Take your choice.*

An easterner who owned a vast library of Western Americana, Clarence Mulford (1883–1956) penned the fictional adventures of Hopalong Cassidy for more than thirty years in numerous short stories and such novels as Hopalong Cassidy *(1912),* Tex *(1922),* Trail Dust *(1934), and* Hopalong Cassidy Serves a Writ *(1941). He also wrote several other novels, including two about a somewhat different type of cowboy hero—*Mesquite Jenkins *(1928) and* Mesquite Jenkins, Tumbleweed *(1932). Much of his short fiction originally appeared in early pulps, most often in* Short Stories, *where "Hopalong Sits In" first saw print in 1929.*

15

*A parenthetical note of interest: in 1951 and 1952 Double-
day published four novels featuring Hoppy, all of them written
by Louis L'Amour under the pseudonym "Tex Burns": Hopalong Cassidy and the Rustlers of West Fork, Hopalong
Cassidy and the Trail to Seven Pines, Hopalong Cassidy
and the Riders of High Rock, and Hopalong Cassidy,
Trouble Shooter. These did not continue the original
Mulford series, but rather portrayed Hoppy as Boyd did on the
screen; Boyd's image, in fact, was used in the cover art, and on
the back of each jacket there were film stills of the actor in his
Cassidy role.*

Hopalong Cassidy dismounted in front of the rough-
boarded hotel, regarding it with a curious detachment which
was the result of a lifetime's experience with such hybrid
affairs. He knew what it would be even before he left the
saddle: saloon, gambling house, and hotel, to mention its
characteristics in the order of their real importance.

Hopalong entered the main room and found that it ran
the full length of the building. A bar paralleled one wall,
card tables filled the open space; and in the inside corner
near the door was a pine desk on which was a bottle of
muddy ink, a corroded pen, a paper-covered notebook of
the kind used in schools for compositions, and a grimy
showcase holding cigars and tobaccos. Behind the desk on
the wall was a short piece of board with nails driven in it, and
on the nails hung a few keys.

A shiftless person with tobacco-stained lips arose from a
nearby table, looking inquiringly at the newcomer.

"Got a room?" asked Hopalong.

"Yeah. Two dollars, in advance," replied the clerk.

"By the week," suggested Hopalong.

"Twelve dollars—we don't count Sundays," said the clerk
with a foolish grin.

"Eat on the premises?" asked the newcomer, sliding a gold
coin across the desk.

The clerk tossed the coin into the air, listened to the ring as it struck the board, tossed it into a drawer, made change, and hooked a thumb over his shoulder.

"Right in yonder," he said, indicating the other half of the building. "Doors open six to eight; twelve to one; six to seven. Pay when you eat an' take what you get. Come with me an' I'll show you the room."

Hopalong obeyed, climbing the steep and economical stairs with just the faintest suggestion of a limp. As they passed down the central hall, he could see into the rooms on each side. They were all alike, even to the arrangement of the furniture. The beds all stood with their heads against the hall wall, in the same relative positions.

"Reckon this will do," he grunted, looking past the clerk into the room indicated. "Stable out back?"

"Yeah. Take yore hoss around an' talk to the stableman," said the clerk, facing around. "Dinner in about an hour."

Hopalong nodded and fell in behind his guide, found the stairs worse in descent than in ascent, and arranged for the care of his horse. When he returned to the room he dropped his blanket roll on the foot of the bed, and then looked searchingly and slowly at the canvas walls. There was nothing to be seen, and shaking his head gently, he went out and down again to wander about the town until time to enter the dining room.

After dinner he saddled his horse and rode down the wide cattle trail, going southward in hope of meeting the SV herd. This was the day it was due; but he was too old a hand to worry about a trail herd being behind time. Johnny Nelson would reach the town when he got there, and there was no reason to waste any thought about the matter. Still, he had nothing else to do, and he pushed on at an easy lope.

He, himself, had been over at Dodge City, where he had learned that Johnny Nelson had a herd on the trail and was bound north. It was a small herd of selected cattle driven by a small outfit. He had not seen Johnny for over a year, and it was too good an opportunity to let pass. For the pleasure of meeting his old friend he had written a letter to him addressed to an important mail station on the new trail, where all outfits called for mail. Some days later he had left Dodge and ridden west, and now he was on hand to welcome the SV owner.

Hopalong passed two herds as he rode, and paused to exchange words with the trail bosses. One of the herds was bound for Wyoming, and the other for Dakota. Trailing had not been very brisk so far this season, but from what the two bosses had heard it was due to pick up shortly. About mid-afternoon Hopalong turned and started back toward town, reaching the hotel soon after the dining-room doors opened.

After supper the town came to life, and as darkness fell, the street was pretty well filled with men. The greater part of the town's population was floating: punchers, gamblers, and others whose occupations were not so well-known.

The main room of the hotel came to life swiftly, the long bar was well lined and the small tables began to fill. The noise increased in volume and it was not long before the place was in full swing. From time to time brawls broke out in the street and made themselves heard; and once pistol shots caused heads to raise and partly stilled the room.

Hopalong sat lazily in a chair between two windows, his back to the wall, placidly engaged in watching the activities about him. More and more his eyes turned to one particular table, where a game of poker was under way, and where the rounds of drinks came in a steady procession. His curiosity was aroused, and he wondered if the situation was the old one.

To find out, he watched to see which player drank the least liquor, and he found that instead of one man doing that, there were two. To a man of Hopalong's experience along the old frontier, that suggested a very pertinent thought; and he watched more keenly now to see if he could justify it.

So far as he was concerned, it was purely an impersonal matter; he knew none of the players and cared nothing who lost in the game. As hand followed hand, and the liquor began to work, the cheating became apparent to him and threatened to become apparent to others; and he found his gorge slowly rising.

Finally one of the players, having lost his last chip and being unable to buy more, pushed back his chair and left the table, reeling toward the street door. Just then, elbowing his way from the crowd at the bar, came one of the trail bosses with whom Hopalong had talked that afternoon. The newcomer stopped behind the vacant chair and gestured toward it inquiringly.

"Shore. Set down," said one of the sober players. The others nodded their acquiescence, soberly or drunkenly as the case might be, and more drinks were ordered. The two sober men had drunk round for round with the others, and yet showed no effects from it. Hopalong flashed a glance at the bar, and nodded wisely. Very likely they were being served tea.

Hopalong pulled his chair out from the wall, tipped it back, and settled down, his big hat slanting well before his eyes. He had ridden all day and was tired, and he found himself drowsing. After an interval, the length of which he did not know, he was aroused to alertness by a shouted curse; but before he could get to his feet or roll off the chair, a shot roared out, almost deafening him. There was a quick flurry at the table, a struggle, and he saw the trail boss, disarmed, being dragged and pushed toward the door. Hopalong removed his sombrero and looked at the hole near the edge of the brim. He was inserting the tip of his little finger into it when one of the players, in a hurried glance around the room, saw the action.

"Close, huh?" inquired the gambler with momentary interest, and then looked around the room again. Several men had pushed out from the crowd and stood waiting in a little group, closely watching the room. As he glimpsed these men, the gambler's face lost its trace of anxiety and he smiled coldly.

Hopalong's eyes flicked from the gambler to the watchful guards and back again, and then he turned slowly to look at the wall behind him, just back of his right ear. The bullet hole was there.

"Yeah, it was close," he said slowly, grinning grimly. "At first I reckoned mebby it might be an old one; but that hole in the wall says it ain't. Who stepped on that fool's pet corn?"

"Nobody; just too much liquor," answered the gambler. "Sometimes it makes a man ugly. Now he's busted up the game, for I shore don't care for a four-hander. Mebby you'd like to take his place?"

"I might," admitted Hopalong with no especial interest. "What you playin', an' how steep?"

"Draw, with jackpots after a full house or better," replied the gambler, looking swiftly but appraisingly at the two drunken players. They had leaned over the table again, and were not to be counted upon to make denials of any statement. "Two bits, an' two dollars; just a friendly game, to pass away the time."

"All right," replied Hopalong, thinking that friendship came rather high in Trailville, if that was the measure of a friendly game.

The gambler waved a hand, and four men stepped to the table. After a moment's argument they took the helpless players from their chairs and started them toward the front door.

Hopalong smiled, thinking that now the game was less than four-handed. He said nothing, however, but stepped forward and dropped into one of the vacant chairs.

"We can get a couple more to take their places," Hopalong said, and nodded gently as his prophecy was fulfilled. He smiled a welcome to the two men and waited until the gambler had taken his own chair. Then Hopalong leaned forward. "You can call me Riordan," he said.

"Kitty out a white chip every game for the house," said the gambler, reaching for the cards. "We play straights between threes and flushes; no fancy combinations. A faced card on the draw can't be taken."

"You playin' for the house?" asked Hopalong needlessly. He was drawing a hand from a pocket as he spoke, and at the gambler's answering nod, he opened the hand and pushed the coins toward the other. "You got chips enough to sell me some," he said.

The game got under way, and the liquor began to arrive. Hopalong was smiling inwardly: he was well fortified to meet the conditions of this game. In the first place, he could stand an amazing amount of whisky; but he did not intend to crowd his capacity by drinking every round. In the second, poker was to him a fine art; and the more dishonest the game, the finer his art—thanks to Tex Ewalt. He always met crookedness with crookedness rather than to cause trouble, but he let the others set the pace.

He looked like a common frontier citizen, with perhaps a month's wages in his pockets, and he believed that was the reason for the moderate limit set by the gambler, who was a tinhorn, and satisfied with small pickings if he could not do better; but as a matter of fact, Hopalong was a full partner in a very prosperous northern ranch, and he could write a check for six figures and have it honored. Last, and fully as important, he was able to take care of himself in any frontier situation from cutting cards to shooting lead. He believed that he was going to thoroughly enjoy his stay in Trailville.

"On the trail?" carelessly asked the gambler as the cards were cut for the first deal.

"No," answered Hopalong, picking up the deck by diagonal corners in case the cards had been shaved. "I'm just driftin' toward home."

As the game went on it appeared that he had a bad poker weakness: every time he had a poor hand and bluffed strongly, his mouth twitched. It took some time for this to register with the others, but when it did, he found that he was very promptly called; and his displeasure in his adversaries' second sight was plain to all who watched.

Along about the middle of the game his mouth must have twitched by accident, for he raked in a pot that had been well built up and leveled up nearly all his loss. The game seesawed until midnight, when it broke up; and Hopalong found that he cashed in twenty dollars less chips than he had bought; twenty dollars' worth of seeds, from which a crop might grow. He knew that he would be a welcomed addition to any poker game in this hotel, that his weaknesses were known, and his consistent and set playing was now no secret.

He went to his room, closed the door, and lighted the lamp, intending to go to bed; but the room was too hot for comfort. There was not a breath of air stirring, and as yet the coolness of the night had not overcome the heat stored up by the walls and roof during the day. He stood for a moment in indecision and then, knowing that another hour would make an appreciable difference in the temperature of the room, he turned and left it, going down to the street.

The night was dark, but star-bright, and he stood for a moment looking about him. The saloons and gambling shacks were going full blast, but they had no appeal for him. He walked toward the corner of the hotel and looked back toward the stables; and then he remembered that he had seen a box against the side wall of the barroom. That was just what he wanted, and he moved slowly along the wall, feeling his way in the deeper shadow, found it, and seated himself with a sigh of relief, leaning back against the wall and relaxing.

Men passed up and down the street, and human voices rose and fell in the buildings along it. Time passed with no attempt on Hopalong's part to keep track of it, but by the deepening chill which comes at that altitude, he believed that the room would now be bearable. About to get up and make a start for the street, he heard and saw two men lazily approach the corner of the building and lean against it, and glance swiftly about them. From the faint light of the front window he thought that he knew who one of them was; and as soon as the man spoke, he was certain of the identity.

"You know what to do," said the speaker. "I looked 'em over good. There's about two hundred head of fine, selected cattle, four-year-olds. It'll be easy to run off most of 'em, or mebby all of 'em. Take 'em round about into Wolf Hollow, an' then scatter 'em to hell an' gone. We'll round 'em up later. Don't bungle it *this* time. Get goin'."

The two men separated, one moving swiftly to where a horse was standing across the street. He mounted quickly and rode away. The other moved out of sight around the corner and disappeared, apparently into the hotel. Three men came past the corner and paused to argue drunkenly; and by the time they had moved on again Hopalong knew that he had lost touch with the man who held his interest.

The coast being clear, Hopalong moved slowly toward the street, went into the barroom and glanced about as he made his way to the stairs. Reaching his room, he closed the door behind him and listened for a few moments. During lulls in the general noise downstairs he could hear a man snoring.

Undressing, he stretched out and gave himself over to a period of quiet but intensive thought. He had nothing positive to go upon; the horseman had ridden off so quickly that he was gone before Hopalong could come to any decision about following him; he realized that by the time he could have saddled up, the man would have been out of reach. He did not know for sure that the two men had referred to the SV herd, nor where to find it if he did know. All he could do was to wait, and to keep his ears open and his wits about him. It would be better to conceal his interest in Johnny Nelson and Johnny's cattle. As a matter of fact he had nothing but unfounded suspicions for the whole structure he was building up.

Back in Dodge City he had been well-informed about Trailville and the conditions obtaining there, since a large percent of the unholy population of Dodge had packed up and gone to the new town. The big herds no longer crossed the Arkansas near the famous old cattle town, to amble up the divide leading to the Sawlog. The present marshal of Dodge was a good friend of Hopalong's, and had been thorough in his pointers and remarks.

Hopalong had learned from him, for one thing, that a good trail herd with a small outfit would be likely to lose cattle and have a deal of trouble before it passed the new town; especially if the trail crew was further reduced in numbers by some of the men receiving time off to enjoy an evening in town. Further than that the marshal had mentioned one man by name, Bradley, and stressed it emphatically; and only tonight Hopalong had heard that man's name called out while the poker game was under way, and had looked with assumed carelessness across the table at the player who had answered to it.

Hopalong had taken pains during the remainder of the evening to be affable to this gentleman, and to study him; he had been so affable and friendly that he even had forborne giving a hint that he knew the gentleman cheated when occasion seemed to warrant it. And this man Bradley was the man he had overheard speak just a few minutes before at the corner of the building.

Perhaps, after all, he would ride down the trail in the morning, if he knew that he was not observed doing it, and try to get in touch with Johnny, even though he did not know how far away the SV herd might be. He knew that the herd had numbered about two hundred head of the best cattle to be found on four ranches; and he knew that the outfit would be small. He feared . . . Ah, hell! What was the use of letting unfounded suspicions make a fool of him, and keep him awake? He turned over on his side and went to sleep like a child.

He was the second man through the dining-room door the next morning. and soon thereafter he left town, bound down the trail, hoping that the SV herd was within a day's ride, and that he could meet it unobserved. He had not covered a dozen miles before he saw a horseman coming toward him up the trail, and something about the man seemed to be familiar. It was not long before he knew the rider to be Bradley.

The two horsemen nodded casually and pulled up, stopping almost leg to leg.

"Leavin' us, Riordan?" asked the upbound man.

"No," answered Hopalong. "The town's dead durin' daylight, an' I figgered to look over the country an' kill some time."

"There ain't nothin' down this way to see," replied the other. "Nor up the other way, neither," he added.

"Ride with you, then, as far as town," said Hopalong, deciding not to show even a single card of his hand.

They went on up the trail at a slow and easy gait, talking idly of this and that, and then Hopalong turned sidewise and asked a question with elaborate casualness.

"Who's town marshal, Bradley?" he asked.

"Slick Cunningham. Why?" asked Bradley, flashing a quick glance at his companion.

Hopalong was silent for a moment, turning the name over in his mind; and then his expression faintly suggested relief.

"Never heard of him," he admitted, and laughed gently, his careless good nature once more restored. "Reckon, accordin' to that, he never heard of me, neither."

"Oh, Slick's all right; he minds his own business purty well," said Bradley, and grinned broadly. "Anyhow, he's out of town right now."

Continuing a purely idle conversation, they soon saw the town off on one side of the trail, and Bradley raised a hand.

"There she is," he said, pulling up. "I've got a couple of errands to do that wouldn't interest you none; so I'll quit you here, an' see you in town tonight."

"Keno," grunted Hopalong, and headed for the collection of shacks that was Trailville. He was halfway to town when he purposely lost his hat. Wheeling, he swung down to scoop it up, and took advantage of the movement to glance swiftly backward; and he was just in time to see Bradley dipping down into a hollow west of the trail. The remainder of the short ride was covered at a walk, and was a thoughtful one.

The day dragged past, suppertime came and went, and again the big room slowly filled with men. Hopalong sat in the same chair, tipped back against the wall, the bullet hole close to his head. Bradley soon came in, stopping at the bar for a few moments, and then led the same group of card players to the same table. Looking around for Hopalong, they espied him, called him by his new name of Riordan, and gestured toward the table. In a few moments the game was under way.

The crowd shifted constantly, men coming and going from and to the street. There was a group bunched at the bar, close to the front door. Two men came in from the street, pushing along the far side of the group, eager to quench their thirst. One of them was Slick Cunningham, town marshal, just back from a special assignment. His name was not even as old as Trailville. He glanced through a small opening in the group to see who was in the room, and as his gaze settled on the men playing cards with Bradley, he stiffened and stepped quickly backward, covered by the group.

"Outside, George," he whispered to his companion. "Pronto! Stand just outside the door an' wait for me!"

George was mildly surprised, but he turned and sauntered to the street, stopping when he reached it.

The marshal was nowhere in sight, but he soon appeared around the corner of the building, and beckoned his friend to his side.

"I just had a good look through the window," he said hurriedly. "I knowed it was him; an' it shore is! When Bradley said he was figgerin' on takin' his pick of that SV herd I told him, an' all of you, too, that he was gettin' ready to pull a grizzly's tail. An' he is! Nelson was one of the old Bar-20 gang. . . . An' who the hell do you reckon is sittin' between Bradley an' Winters, playin' poker with 'em? Hopalong Cassidy! Hopalong Cassidy, damn his soul!"

"Thought you said he was up in Montanny?" replied George, with only casual interest.

"He was! But, great Gawd! he don't have to stay there, does he? You get word to Bradley, quick as you can. Settin' elbow to elbow with Cassidy! If that don't stink, then I don't know what does! Cassidy here in Trailville, an' Nelson's cattle comin' up the trail! I'm tellin' you that somethin's wrong!"

"You reckon he knows anything?" asked George, to whom the name of Hopalong Cassidy did not mean nearly so much as it did to his companion.

"Listen!" retorted the marshal earnestly, "Nobody on Gawd's gray earth knows how much that feller knows! I've never run up ag'in him yet when he didn't know a damn sight more than I wanted him to; an' what he don't know, he damn soon finds out. You get word to Bradley. I'm pullin' out of town, an' I'm stayin' out till this mess is all cleaned up. If Cassidy sees me, he'll know that I know him; an' if he knows that I know him, he'll know that I'll pass on the word to my friends. I'll give a hundred dollars to see him buried."

"You mean that?" asked George, with sudden interest.

Slick peered into his eyes through the gloom, and then snorted with disgust.

"Don't you be a damn fool!" he snapped. "I didn't say that I wanted to see *you* buried, did I?"

"Hell with that!" retorted George. "I'm askin' you if you really mean that as an offer; if you'll pay a hundred dollars to the man that kills him?"

"Well, I didn't reckon nobody would be fool enough to take me up," said Slick, but he suddenly leaned forward again, as a new phase of the matter struck him. "Yes, you damn fool! Yes, I will!" He pulled his hat down firmly and nodded. "My share of that herd money will come to a lot more than a hundred dollars; but if that pizen pup stays alive around here we won't steal a head, an' I won't get a cent. Yes, the offer goes; but you better get help, an' split it three ways. There's only one man in town who would have any kind of a chance, an' his name ain't George."

"I'll take care of that end of it," replied George, "an' now I'm goin' in to get word to Bradley. So long."

"So long," said Slick, and forthwith disappeared around the corner on his way to the little corral behind the marshal's office. There was a good horse in that corral, and a horse was just what he wanted at the moment.

George pushed through the group, signaled to the bartender, ordered a drink, and whispered across the counter. Placing his glass on the bar, George moved carelessly down the room, nodding to right and left. He stopped beside the busy poker table, grunted a greeting to the men he knew, and dragged up a chair near Bradley's right elbow, where he could look at the cards in his friend's hand, and by merely raising his eyes, look over their tops at the player on the left.

Hopalong had dropped out for that deal, and was leaning back in his chair, his eyes shaded by the brim of his hat. His placid gaze was fixed on the window opposite and he was wondering whose face it was that he had glimpsed in the little patch of light outside. The face had been well back, and the beams of light from the lamps had not revealed it well; but it was something to think about, and, having nothing else to do at the moment, he let his mind dwell on it. He did not like faces furtively peering in through lighted windows.

Bradley chuckled, pulled in the pot and tossed his cards unshown into the discard.

"Hello, George," he said, turning to smile at the man on his right.

"Hello, Bill. Won't nobody call yore hand tonight?"

"They don't call me at the right time," laughed Bradley, in rare good humor. "This seems to be my night." He looked up at the man who now stepped into his circle of vision. "What is it, Tom?"

"Bartender wants to see you, Bill. Says it's important, an' won't take more'n a minute."

"Deal me out this hand," said Bradley, pushing back his chair and following the messenger.

Hopalong let the cards lay as they fell, and when the fifth had dropped in front of him his fingers pushed them into a neat, smooth-sided book, and he watched the faces of the other players as the hands were picked up. The house gambler was in direct line with that part of the bar where Bradley had stopped, and Hopalong's gaze, lifting from the face of the player, for a moment picked out Bradley and the bartender. The latter was looking straight at him and the expression on the man's face was grim and hostile. Hopalong looked at the next player, lifted his own cards and riffled the corners to let the pips flash before his eyes.

"She's open," said the man on the dealer's left, tossing a chip into the center of the table.

"Stay," grunted Hopalong, doing likewise in his turn. A furtive face at the window, a message for Bradley, and a suddenly hostile bartender—and Johnny's herd was small, selected, and had a small outfit with it. Suspicions, suspicions, always suspicions! He bent his head, and then raised it quickly and looked at George before that person had time to iron out his countenance. From that instant Hopalong did not like George, and determined to keep an eye on him.

Bradley returned, slapped George on the shoulder, and drew up to the table, watching the play. Not once did he look at Hopalong.

When the play came around to Hopalong it had been raised twice, and that person, studying his cards intently, suddenly looked over their tops and tossed them away. Bradley's expression changed a flash too late.

"They ain't runnin' for me," growled Hopalong, glancing from Bradley to George. "Game's gettin' tiresome, but I'll try a few more hands."

"Hell!" growled Bradley, affable and smiling again. "That ain't the trouble—the game's too small to hold a feller's interest."

"Right!" quickly said the house gambler, nodding emphatically as he sensed a kill. "Too tee-totally damn small! Let's play a round of jackpots to finish this up; an' then them that don't want to play for real money can't say they was throwed out cold."

"I'll set out the round of jacks an' come in on the new game," said Hopalong, risking quick glances around the room. No one seemed to be paying any particular attention to him.

"Me, too. No, I'll give you fellers a chance," said Bradley.

"Don't need to give me no chance," said a player across from him. "I'm ready for the big game."

Hopalong saw a young man push through the crowd near the door and head straight for the table. As he made his way down the room he was the cynosure of all eyes, and a ripple of whispered comment followed him. Hopalong did not know it, but the newcomer was a killer famous for his deeds around Trailville—a man who would kill for money, who had always "got" his man, and who was a close friend of Bradley's.

"Hello, Bill," the newcomer addressed Bradley, and then dropped into the chair which George surrendered to him, as if he was expected to do so; and thereupon George moved toward the bar and was lost to sight.

Bradley nodded, smiled and faced the table again, gesturing with both hands.

"Riordan, meet Jim Hawes. Jim, Riordan's a stranger here."

The two men exchanged nods, sizing each other up. Hawes saw a typical cowpuncher, past middle age; but a man whose deeds rang from one edge of the cattle country to the other; a man whose reputation would greatly enhance that of anybody who managed to kill him with a gun in an even break. His mantle of fame would rest automatically upon the shoulders of his master.

Hopalong saw a vicious-faced killer, cold, unemotional, and of almost tender years. There was a swagger in his every movement and one could easily see that he was an important individual. The young man's eyes were rather close together, and his chin receded. To Hopalong, both of these characteristics were danger marks. He had found, in his own experience, that the prognathous jaw is greatly overrated. Hawes reminded him of a weasel.

"Haven't had a game for a long time," said Hawes, speaking with almost pugnacious assurance. "Reckon I'll set in an' give her a whirl."

"She's goin' to be a real one, Jim," said the house dealer uneasily. His profession, to his way of thinking, called for a little trickery with the cards upon occasion; but with Jim Hawes in the game only an adept would dare attempt it; not so much that Hawes was capable of detecting fine work, but because he would shoot with as little compunction as a rattler strikes.

"I like 'em big; the bigger the better," boasted Hawes, his cold eyes on Hopalong. "What you say, Riordan?" he asked, and the way he said the words made them a challenge. It appeared that his humor was not a pleasant one tonight.

"I'd rather have 'em growed up," replied Hopalong, looking him in the eyes, "*Well* growed up," amended Hopalong, his gaze unswerving.

Somewhere in the room a snicker sounded, quickly hushed as Hawes glanced toward the sound. The room had grown considerably quieter, ears functioning instead of tongues, and this, in itself, was a hint to an observing man. Hawes's gaze was back again like a flash, and he kept it set on the stranger's face while he slowly, with his left hand, drew his chair closer to the table, in the space provided for him by Bradley. He, too, sensed the quiet of the room, and a tight, knowing smile wreathed his thin lips.

"We'll make it growed up enough for you, Mister Riordan," he said, his left hand now drawing a roll of bills from a pocket. "How's five, an' twenty?" he challenged.

"Cents or dollars?" curiously asked Hopalong, his face expressionless.

Hawes flushed, but checked the fighting words before they reached his teeth.

"What makes *you* reckon it might be cents?" he demanded, triumphantly.

"Just had a feelin' that it might be," calmly answered Hopalong. "Either one is a waste of time."

Bradley raised his eyebrows, regarding the speaker intently.

"Yeah?" he softly inquired. "How do you grade a growed-up game?"

"It all depends on who I'm playin' with," answered Hopalong, his eyes on Hawes's tense face.

"Five an' fifty—*dollars!*" snapped the youth, showing his teeth.

"She's improvin' with every word," chuckled the house player.

"Damn near of age, anyhow," said Hopalong, nodding. "Straight draw poker? Threes, straights, flushes, an' so forth? No fancy hands?"

"The same game we have been playin'," said the house player. "Jackpots after full houses, or better. That suit everybody?"

Silence gave consent, the chips were redeemed at the old figure, deftly stacked and counted by the house player, and resold at the new prices. Hopalong drew out a roll of dirty bills, peeled off two of them, and with them bought a thousand dollars' worth of chips. He placed the remainder of the roll on the table near the chips and nodded at it.

"When that's gone, I'm busted," he said, and looked at Hawes.

"Oh, don't worry! There's mine," sneered the youth, and bought the same amount of counters. Inwardly he thrilled; in so steep a game, cheating would be a great temptation to anyone inclined that way; and a crooked play would be justification for what followed it, and would suit him as well as any other excuse.

The player who had announced that he was ready for the bigger game now raised both hands toward heaven, pushed back his chair, and motioned grandiloquently toward the table; but no one in the room cared to take his place: the game was far too steep for them, and they sensed a deadly atmosphere.

"Quittin' us, Frank?" asked Bradley, with a knowing grin.

"Cold an' positive! My money comes harder than your'n, Bradley; an' I ain't got near as much of it. No, sir! I'll get all the excitement I'll need, just settin' back and watchin' the play."

He had been sitting on Hopalong's left, and when he withdrew from the game, he pulled his chair back from the table, and now he drew it farther out of the way. Hopalong shifted in that direction, to even up the spacing; but as he stopped, he sensed Bradley's nearness, and saw that the latter had moved after him, but too far. Bradley's impetus had carried him even closer to Hopalong than he had been before. Bradley smiled apologetically and moved back, but only for a few inches. The fleeting expression of Hawes's face revealed satisfaction, and dressed the blundering shift with intent. What intent? In Hopalong's mind there could be only one; and that one, deadly.

The game got under way, and it was different from the more or less innocent affair which had preceded it. It was different in more ways than one. In the first place there was now present a thinly veiled hostility, an atmosphere of danger. In the second, a man could bluff with more assurance; a player would think twice before he would toss in fifty dollars to call a hand when he, himself, held little. In the third, a clever card manipulator would be tempted to make use of his best-mastered tricks of sleight of hand; and should any man call for a new deck, or palm the old one for a moment, it would be well to give thought to the possible substitution of a cold deck. Here was the kind of game Hopalong could enjoy; he had cut his teeth on them, and had been given excellent instruction by a past master of the game. Tex Ewalt had pronounced him proficient.

The first few hands were more in the nature of skirmishes, for with the change in the stakes had come a change in the style of play. Hopalong's fingers were calloused, but the backs of his fingers were not; and he now bunched his cards in his left hand, face to the palm, and let the backs of the fingers of his right hand brush gently down the involved patterns, searching for pin pricks. As the cards were dealt to him, Hopalong idly pushed them about on the table, to get a different slant of lamplight on each one. If the polish had been removed by abrasives or acids the reflected light would show it.

At last came a jackpot, and it was passed three times, growing greatly in the process. The house player picked up the cards to deal, shuffling them swiftly, and ruffled them together with both hands hiding them. He pushed the deck toward Hopalong for the cut, in such a manner that if the latter chose the easier and more natural movement, he would cut with his nearest, or left, hand. If he did this, his fingers would naturally grasp the sides of the deck, and not the ends; and if the cards were trimmed, such a cut might well be costly.

As the dealer took his hand off the deck, Hopalong let his left hand reach for his cigarette; and it being thus occupied, and quite innocently so, he reached across his body with the idle right and quite naturally picked up the upper part of the deck by the ends. The dealer showed just the slightest indication of annoyance at this loss of time, and, finding Hopalong's bland gaze on the cards, forewent switching the cut, and dealt them as they lay.

Hawes opened for ten dollars. Bradley saw and raised it only five. Hopalong qualified. The dealer saw, and Hawes saw Bradley's raise, and boosted the limit. The others dropped out. Hawes showed his openers and took the pot. As the play went on, Hopalong observed a strange coincidence. The ante was five dollars; the limit, fifty. Every time that Hawes opened for ten dollars, and Bradley raised it five, or Bradley opened for ten, and Hawes raised it five, the opener thereupon boosted the limit when his time came, and very often dropped out on the next round to let the other win. Here was team work: Hawes and Bradley vs. all.

Hopalong glanced inquiringly at the house player, and caught an almost imperceptible wink directed at himself. There was no need for these two men to go into conference where teamwork was concerned; they knew how to join forces without previous agreements. And now, teamwork was called for as a matter of self-preservation.

The play went on without much action, and Hawes picked up the cards, bunching them for the deal. He was not an expert, and a dozen men in the room saw the clumsy switch, and held their breaths; but nothing violent happened. Apparently the other three players had not seen anything of interest. Bradley opened for ten dollars. Hopalong, looking at his cards, saw three kings and a pair of tens. He passed, and smiled inwardly at the dealer's poorly concealed look of amazement. The house player saw, but when both Hawes and Bradley had raised the limit in turn, he threw his hand in the discard and watched Bradley take the pot by default.

Hopalong, toying idly with his cards, now looked at them again, and swore loudly and bitterly.

"Damn fool! I thought it was two pairs . . . Will you *look* at *that?*"

Hopalong's outspread cards revealed their true worth,

and the house player chuckled deep in his throat, his eyes beaming with congratulations.

"Pat king full," he said. "Well, Riordan, it can be beat."

"It can," admitted Hopalong, trying to smile. For an instant the two men looked understandingly into each other's eyes.

There was now no question about the status of this game. Both Hopalong and the house player had seen the clumsy switch; and it had been followed by a pat king full. The bars were now down and the rules were up. It was just a case of outcheating cheaters, and the devil take the less adept.

On Bradley's deal Hawes took another small pot by default, and Hopalong picked up the cards. His big hands moved swiftly, his fingers flicking almost in a blur of speed. The house player watched him, and then, curiously, against his habit, picked up each card as it fell in front of him. Seven, five, eight, and six of hearts. The fifth card seemed to intrigue him greatly: with it he would get the measure of a dexterous player's real mentality; and he hoped desperately that he would not have to play a pat hand. He sighed, picked up the card, and saw the jack of clubs. For a moment he regarded the dealer thoughtfully, and almost affectionately, and then he swiftly made up his mind. He would risk one play for the sake of knowledge. He opened for a white chip.

Hawes saw, and raised a red. Bradley stayed. Hopalong dropped out. The house player saw, and raised a blue, a true mark of confidence in a stranger's dealing ability; and almost before the chips had struck the table, Hawes saw and raised the limit. Bradley stayed, and the house player, rubbing his chin thoughtfully, evened it up, and asked for one card. He looked at it and turned it over, face up on the table. It was the four of hearts.

"Thanks," he said, nodding to Hopalong. "I needed that. It costs fifty dollars to play with me," he said to the others.

Hawes thought swiftly. As a heart, the card would fill a flush; as a four spot, it would build up three of a kind, a straight, a full house, or four of a kind. Had it been a jack he would have hesitated; but now he tried to hide his elation, and tossed in a hundred dollars to see and to raise. Bradley sighed and dropped out.

"You took two cards," murmured the house player thoughtfully. "Mebby—mebby you got another; but I doubt it. She's up ag'in."

"Once more," said Hawes, his eyes glinting.

"Well, it's my business to know a bluff when I see one," said the house player, studying his adversary. "It's my best judgment that you . . . Well, anyhow, I'll back it, Hawes, an' boost her once more."

"*Gracias!*" laughed Hawes, a little tensely. "When I went to school a four spot was a right small card. See you, an' raise ag'in."

"An' once more."

"Ag'in."

"Once more."

"Ag'in."

"An' once more," said the house player. "I allus like to play a hand like this clean to the end. They're right scarce."

Suddenly Hawes had a disturbing suspicion. Could it be that his opponent had held four of a kind pat? He, himself, had thrown away an ace and a queen. That left two possible high fours: kings or jacks. He looked at his own cards, and decided that he had pressed them for all they were worth.

"Then show it to me!" he growled, calling.

"It's the gambler's prayer," said the house player, laying down his cards slowly and one by one. The five of hearts joined the face-up four; then the six, and then the seven. He looked calmly over the top of the last card, holding it close to his face; and then, sighing, placed it where it belonged, and dropped both hands under the edge of the table.

"Straight flush," he said calmly.

Hawes flushed and then went pale. Both of his hands were on the table, while the house player's were out of sight. He swore in his throat and started to toss his cards into the discard, but the house player checked him.

"It's a showdown, Hawes. I paid as much to see your hand as you paid to see mine. Turn 'em over."

Hawes obeyed, slamming the cards viciously, and four pleasant ten-spots lay in orderly array.

"Hard luck for a man to git a hand like that at the wrong time," said the winner.

He drew in the chips and picked up the cards. A thought passed through his mind: when playing with keen, smart men, a foolish play will often win. In such a case, two successive bluffs often pay dividends. The house player chuckled in his throat.

"Jacks to open this one," the house player—it was his deal—announced as Hopalong cut. It pleased him to see the way in which Hopalong followed the natural way to cut the deck, and lifted it by the sides; but it only showed confidence, because the dealer wanted no cut at all, and switched it perfectly as he took it up again. In what he was about to do, he would accomplish two things: he would return a favor, and also help Hawes into the situation the latter had been looking for. To make plain his own innocence in the matter, he talked while he dealt.

"The art of cuttin' cards is a fine one," he said. "You hear a lot about slick dealin', but hardly a word about slick cuttin'. That's because it's mighty rare. Why, once I knowed a feller that could cut . . . Oh, well. I'll tell that story after the hand is played."

But it so happened that the house player never told that lie.

Hawes passed. Bradley opened for ten. Hopalong stayed, and the dealer dropped out. Hawes raised it five and Bradley tossed in a blue and a white chip, seeing, and raising the limit. Hopalong leveled up and added another blue. Hawes dropped out. Bradley studied his hand and saw. He drew two cards and Hopalong took one. The latter would have been very much surprised if he had been disappointed, for he had detected the switched cut. Bradley pushed out a blue chip, and Hopalong saw and raised another. Bradley pushed in two, and Hopalong two more. Back and forth it went, time after time.

Hawes leaned over and looked at Bradley's hand. He studied Hopalong a moment, and gave thought to the straight flush he had just had the misfortune to call. Straight flushes do not come two in a row—at least, that was so in his experience. He leaned forward, his left hand resting on his piled chips.

"Side bet, Riordan?" he inquired sneeringly.

"How much?" asked Hopalong, a little nervously.

"How much you got?" snapped Hawes.

"Plenty."

"Huh! Dollars, or *cents?*" sneered Hawes, quoting an unpleasant phrase.

"Dollars. Lemme see. Five, ten, fifteen, twenty, twenty-five, thirty, thirty-five, forty, forty-one, two, three, four, five, six—forty-six hundred, leavin' me ham an' aig money. You scared?"

"Scared, hell!" snapped Hawes. He counted his own resources, found them greatly short, and looked inquiringly at Bradley. "Lend me the difference?" he asked.

Bradley nodded, and beckoned to the head bartender.

"Give Hawes what he needs, an' put a memo in the safe," he ordered.

In a few moments the game went on, the side bets lying apart from the pot. Then Bradley, grinning triumphantly, raised the limit again, certain that Riordan did not have money enough left to meet it. It was a sucker trick, but sometimes it worked.

Hopalong looked at him curiously, hesitated, went through his pockets, and then turned a worried face to his adversary.

"Anybody in the room lend me fifty dollars?" he asked,

loudly; and not a voice replied. Hawes's malignant gaze swept the crowd and held it silent. Not a man dared to comply with the request.

"Is that the way you win yore pots, Bradley?" asked Hopalong coldly.

"I've raised you. Call or quit."

Hopalong's right hand dug down into a pocket, and he laughed nastily as he dropped a fifty-dollar bill on top of the chips in the center of the table.

"What you got, tinhorn?" he asked.

"I got the gambler's second prayer," chuckled Bradley, exposing four aces, and reaching for the pot.

"But I got the first," grunted Hopalong. "Same little run of hearts that we saw before."

For a moment there was an utter silence, and then came a blur of speed from Hawes, but just the instant before it came, Bradley fell off his chair to the left, his own left arm falling across Hopalong's right forearm, blocking a draw; but other men had discovered, when too late, that Hopalong's left hand was the better of the two. The double roar seemed to bend the walls, and sent the lamp flames leaping, to flicker almost to extinction. One went out, the other two recovered. The smoke thinned to show Hawes sliding from his chair, and Bradley on the floor where he had fallen by his own choice, with both hands straining at the Mexican spur which spiked his cheek.

The two leveled Colts held the crowd frozen in curious postures. Hands were raised high, or held out well away from belts. Hopalong backed to the wall, his left-hand gun still smoking. He felt the wall press against him, and then he nodded swiftly to the house player.

"You had a hell of a lot to say about the cut, after you switched it! Now let's see what you know about a *draw*!" As Hopalong spoke, he shoved both guns into their sheaths, and slowly crossed his arms.

The gambler made no move, scarcely daring to breathe. He still doubted his senses.

"All right, then. Get out, an' stay out!" ordered Hopalong, and as the house player passed through the door, another man came in; a man unsteady on his feet, and covered with sweat and dust and blood.

The newcomer leaned against the bar for a moment, his gaze searching the room; and as he saw his old friend, Hopalong Cassidy, his old friend recognized him. It was Johnny Nelson.

"Hoppy!" he called, joyously.

"Johnny! What's up?"

"They rushed us in the dark, an' shot all of us up. Not seriously, but we're out of action. They got every head—near two hundred!"

Johnny Nelson's gaze wavered, rested for an instant on the open window to one side of his friend, and across the room from him; and, vague and unsteady as he was, he yielded to the gunman's instinct. His right hand dropped, and twisted up like a flash to the top of the holster, and the crash of his shot became a scream in the night outside the open window. George had lost his hundred-dollar fee—and with it, his life.

"Pullin' down on you, from the dark, Hoppy; but I got the skunk," muttered Johnny. He leaned against the bar again and took the whisky which an ingratiating bartender placed under his nose. "They got 'em all. Hoppy—near two hundred head."

Hopalong had his back to the wall again, both guns out and raised for action.

"Good kid!" he called. "I just made a trade with the fellers that stole your cattle. They can keep the steers, and we'll keep the poker winnin's I made by outcheating them two cheaters. Two hundred head at near thirty dollars apiece, kid—which gives you a bigger profit, an' saves you twelve hundred miles of trailin'. Watch the room, kid." He raised his hand. "Bartender, cash in them chips at five, ten, and fifty. *Pronto!*"

It did not take long to turn the counters into money, and Hopalong, backing past the table and toward his capable friend, picked up his winnings, jammed them into a pocket, and slowly reached the stair door.

"It's a tight corner, kid," said Hopalong crisply. "But yore in no shape to ride. Up them stairs, in front of me." He stepped aside for his friend to pass, and then he stepped back again, his foot feeling for the first tread. His gaze flicked about the room, and he smiled thinly.

"My name's Cassidy," he said, and the smile now twisted his hard face. "My friends call me Hopalong. When I go to bed, I go to sleep. Any objections?"

The spellbound silence was broken by murmurs of surprise. Several faces showed quick friendliness, and a man in a far corner slowly got to his feet.

"An old friend of your'n is a right good friend of mine, Cassidy," he said, glancing slowly and significantly around the room. "Anybody that can't wait for daylight will taste my lead. Good night, you old hoss-thief!"

"Good night, friend," said Hopalong. The door slowly closed, and the crowd listened to the accented footsteps of a slightly lame, red-haired gentleman who made his unhurried way upward.

The man in the corner licked his lips and looked slowly around again.

"An' I meant what I said," he announced, and sat down to find his glass refilled.

DOAN WHISPERS

William MacLeod Raine

SHORT-SHORTS were not common in the Western pulps. For one thing, readers—and therefore editors—preferred longer stories; for another, writers were paid by the word, often at the rate of one cent or less, and could not afford to indulge in miniflights of the imagination. Good short-shorts did occasionally get written and published, however, and the best of them packed a well-rounded story into very few words. "Doan Whispers," which originally appeared in Short Stories *in 1932, is a sterling example.*

William MacLeod Raine (1871–1954) was a major name in the popular Western field during the first half of this century. In his fifty-year career he published 81 Western novels, notably Wyoming *(1908),* Steve Yeager *(1915),* Rutledge Trails the Ace of Spades *(1930), and* Run of the Brush *(1936); numerous short stories and articles; and four nonfiction books on Western history, the best known of which is* Famous Sheriffs and Western Outlaws *(1929). Although English-born, he was raised in the West, worked on a cattle ranch, and numbered rustlers, lawmen, and gamblers among his acquaintances. His fiction had an authentic ring as a result.*

"There's one way," Steve Corcoran said. "I could shoot it out with him."

Doan grinned at the big brown man. "So you could, Steve, and go to work for the State of Texas afterward—if he didn't bump you off."

"I reckon he'd get me," Corcoran admitted regretfully. "I

never was any hand with a six-gun, and he's sudden death with one."

"We're not going to waste you on an even break with riffraff like Buck Ormsby. Anyhow, those days are past. Maybe you've been so busy watching Buck's herd grow, Steve, that you haven't noticed the law has come into the land. Little red schoolhouses are in. Guns are out."

The big cattleman frowned at his friend's levity. Doan was a chirrupy little fellow with a face like a wrinkled winter pippin. Black eyes, sharp as gimlets, met Corcoran's grim look.

"What's the sense of talking about law?" Corcoran exploded. "We both know he's rustling 3 C stock. Everybody knows it. When he grins at me he's practically bragging about it. Do you expect me to sit like a buzzard on a cottonwood while he steals me blind?"

"I expect you to use what horse sense you have, if any," Doan told him cheerfully.

"I've been using it. D'you want me to hunt him down and string him to a tree?"

"No, Steve. We're not in Billy the Kid's days. I mentioned law a while ago."

"I heard you. You're like a parrot that has learned two words. All I hear from you is 'No good' when I suggest anything."

"I'll say something else. Down at the store I heard your boy Bob was allowing to get married."

Corcoran surveyed him with disgust. "What's that got to do with getting rid of Buck Ormsby?"

"It would be a nice present to start the boy with a brand of his own. A bunch of good fat calves would run into money after a while."

"Doan, I'm not figuring on how to give my calves away, but how to keep them."

Doan offered for consideration another apparently irrelevant remark. "Ormsby is going down to Santone to ride in the rodeo. He'll be away all week."

"Does that buy us anything?"

The eyes in Doan's face were brighter than usual. He hitched his chair forward and talked steadily in a low voice that was almost a whisper. Corcoran listened attentively. When Doan had finished he slapped a big hand on his thigh.

"We've got him!" the big man cried. "He can laugh at law and bluff out threats. He's too bullheaded to be scared of gunplay. But he can't fight this. He's beat."

Buck Ormsby roped and saddled a claybank with an economy of effort that certified efficiency. He was a lank, lean man, tough as hickory. In his cold eyes, there was always a vigilant wolf look.

He had done very well at San Antonio. First prize for roping, third for bulldogging, was not so bad. Things were looking his way. Two years ago he had been down to the blanket. Now he had a thousand dollars in his pocket and a herd of good stuff increasing a lot faster than the law allows. It had been a good idea for him to take over Peterson's little mountain ranch. A man who hustled could get rich quick when he neighbored a big outfit like Corcoran's 3 C.

The 3 C brand had been made to order for him, he reflected. Two little touches of a running iron converted it into the B O. When he had registered his initials as a brand Buck had had in mind the proximity of Corcoran's herd. The few scrubs with which he had started as a nucleus were the most remarkable mothers ever known in the district. His calf crop was about nine hundred percent a year.

At a road gait Buck jogged down the highway. He was pleasantly aware that this is a good world for the man on horseback who swings a wide loop. You had to have brains and nerve. Well, he had both.

Two riders topped a rise in the road and moved toward

him. Buck grinned and made sure casually his gun was handy. He did not expect to use it, but a fellow never could tell. The horsemen were Corcoran and Doan.

He drew up and rested his weight easily on one stirrup. "How's everything on the range?" he asked impudently. "I been down to Santone."

The answer of Corcoran boomed out cheerfully. "Fine. Looks like we'll have a good season, Buck."

The rustler was surprised. This was not the way Corcoran had spoken to him the last time they met.

"Good calf crop for the 3 C?" he inquired insolently.

"Not so good," the owner of the brand admitted. "But I reckon I'll make up somewhere else what I lose there. A fellow oughtn't to put all his eggs into one basket, Buck. If he does, and stubs his toe, where's he at?"

Ormsby did not knew what that meant. He was still puzzling over it when he took the hill trail from the road. What had that little cuss Doan been chuckling about?

Buck's keen eyes picked up a little bunch of cattle in a draw. He rode down to have a look at the stock. A calf on the outskirts carried a brand he did not know. Buck scratched his head. This was a new one on him. The calf must have traveled far. No outfit within fifty miles had such a brand. Queer, too. He did not find a cow in the bunch marked that way.

He went on his way. He saw another calf with the new brand—and another—and another. Then he caught sight of two together.

Where in Mexico were his B O calves? An uneasy suspicion jumped to his mind. He roped and threw a calf.

With a savage curse he rose to his feet. Buck did not need to investigate further to know that he had been put out of business, that he had nothing left but the scrub cows with which he had started. This was Corcoran's work, of course. While Buck had been away at San Antonio the 3 C riders had held a roundup. Every B O calf on the range had been branded B O B in a box.

He was beaten. No matter how fast his running iron changed the 3 C to B O, within a week the cowpunchers of Corcoran would turn the B O into the new brand—B O B in a box.

"Reckon I better drift to Arizona," Buck Ormsby said ruefully. "An honest rustler doesn't get a break in this country."

SWINDLE AT PIUTE SINK

Luke Short

SOME critics seem to believe that Western pulp fiction was restricted to conventional stories of roving cowboys, steely-eyed lawmen, and cold-hearted gunslingers. The entries in this anthology surely prove otherwise. Stories in the Western pulps had a broad range of backgrounds, of heroes and heroines, of subject matter. Harry F. Olmsted, for instance, wrote a series of excellent novelettes for Dime Western *in the early forties that are set in Alta California and feature a tough-minded Franciscan monk named Friar Robusto. And Luke Short, among others, wrote often and well of miners, mining, and gold and siver boom camps and the men who inhabited them—men such as assayer Ames Littlepage, the hero of "Swindle at Piute Sink."*

The stories and novels of Luke Short (Frederick Glidden, 1908–1975) were anything but conventional pulp fare. Rich in character, incident, factual data, and an authentic flavor of the Old West, they represent some of the best popular Western fiction written from the midthirties to the midseventies. Short's first pulp yarns appeared in Cowboy Stories *in 1935; his first novel,* Feud at Single Shot, *was published in 1936. Among his other 62 novels are such classics as* Gunman's Chance *(1941), the basis for the memorable film* Blood on the Moon, *with Robert Mitchum;* And the Wind Blows Free *(1945),* Vengeance Valley *(1950),* First Campaign *(1965), and a trio of first-rate books about miners and mining—*Hard Money *(1940),* Silver Rock *(1953), and* Rimrock *(1955). He also edited four very good Western anthologies in the fifties, among them the first volume of stories by the Western Writers of America,* Bad Men and Good *(1953). A recent posthumous collection,* Luke Short's Best of the West *(1983), does not* *include "Swindle at Piute Sink," which is reprinted here for the first time since its original 1939 publication in* Western Story.

Ames Littlepage, having yanked down his window blind in the hope of shutting out the heat of early evening and the mingled smells from the reduction mills, turned to contemplate the pleated-bosom shirt on his bed. Naked to the waist, jangling two buttons in his large, half-closed fist, he reflected that he was probably a composite picture of all single men an hour before a party.

When he put on his coat over thick, powerfully muscled shoulders, it was with a sheepish feeling. Downstairs Mrs. Donovan was laying out a second supper for the Union Consolidated men who had seven miles to ride from the mine after the six o'clock shift took over.

Phil Michelson, one of the crew, good-naturedly growled, "Hello, lucky," to Ames. It was the greeting of a hungry man who has waited too long for food, to one who has already been fed; and Ames, understanding it, grinned as he pushed through the door into the kitchen. His long, angular face, glowing after his shave, was a curious mixture of toughness and reflection, the face of a philosopher too young, too big, too active to be guided entirely by the obvious verities.

Lily Donovan was kneading tomorrow's bread on the large kitchen table, her arms almost to the elbows in the yeasty dough. She was trying to push a wisp of wheat-colored hair out of her face with her shoulder as Ames came to stand just inside the door, his shape tall and thick.

"Lily," he said, a slightly embarrassed grin on his long face, "have you got a needle and thread—white thread?" And then when he realized what his interruption meant, he said quickly, "No, no, I don't need it now."

Lily laughed. "Buttons?" Her voice had a pleasant, friendly lilt.

"Yes."

"You'll have to wait a minute and I'll sew them on for you."

Ames settled his shoulder against the wall to wait, and Lily, glancing at him, said, "You might bring the shirt down."

Ames went upstairs, got it and came down again. Lily was drying her hands on the towel that hung above the sink. She took the shirt from him and he followed her out onto the side porch, which held only a small cot and her bureau, lighted by a bracket lamp on the wall. About her clung the good smell of yeasty bread, and Ames wondered idly if the reason her slim back was held as straight as a gun barrel was nature's compensation for the hours she spent in the quiet, uncomplaining drudgery.

He leaned against the door frame. "This isn't right," he declared apologetically. "Room and board doesn't include patching up what a Chinaman butchers."

"You should buy some shirts," Lily said, bringing out her sewing basket and sitting down on the cot.

Ames watched her curiously as she looked first at the shirt collar, then at the cuffs.

"These need turning," she remarked. He said nothing and then she ran her hand up the sleeve. Two square inches of her palm showed through a hole in the forearm of the shirt and she looked questioningly at him. Her eyes were blue, younger than his gray ones, but wiser, and there was a friendliness in her mouth that was teasing and yet almost manlike. "And what about this?" she asked.

Ames laughed then. "No one will see it unless we play poker. And if they start poker, I say good-by."

"I can patch it."

"No, I'll slop acid on it again tomorrow, so why bother?" He paused, frowning a little. "Besides, I mean that about the poker."

"They say you can take care of yourself." Lily said, not looking up from threading her needle.

"Not with that crowd," Ames said shortly. "There's Haleman from the Piute Mills. He won't play under a fifty dollar limit. And Herkenhoff and Wieboldt and that Pacific Shares crowd. They're owners. An assayer hasn't got any business bucking that kind of money."

"You can some day, Ames," Lily told him.

"You think so?" Ames asked quickly.

Lily smiled, but did not look up from her sewing. "What does your Cornelia think? Would she marry a man who couldn't protect himself among her own friends?"

Ames grinned faintly, and shook his head. "She has faith, all right, but damned little understanding, Lily. Being rich, she can't comprehend poverty." He paused, watching her swift fingers sew on the buttons. "But you," he went on slowly, "you're poor, and you know that poor people stay poor. And still you can encourage me."

Lily shrugged. "Rich men like you, Ames. That's all it takes in a boom town like this."

When she was finished he thanked her, smiling, and went upstairs to put on his shirt. He came down again almost immediately, his boots holding a dull polish, his black suit clean, his black hat brushed free of the mica dust that was a part of the air of this town. Lily, who was clearing the table after the last diners, waved and smiled to him as he went out.

The Donovans' boardinghouse lay just a block from the rutted main street of Piute Sink, and as Ames turned into it the color and noise and bustle stirred him. It was a bawdy, brawling town that talked of gold and shares, of melons and dividends and the stock market, of claims and pumps and judgments, of high-grade stuff, borrasca and bonanzas, of stock rigging and mine rigging—but mostly of gold.

It was young enough so that civic pride had not yet forced the huge, ten-team ore wagons to use the back streets on the way from the mines in the mountains beyond to the reduction mills; and yet it was old enough to contain a three-story brick hotel that stood less than a hundred yards from tent saloons.

Millions of dollars of the big money in San Francisco had been poured into Piute Sink's mines, its mills and their equipment, and still a man could not walk a block of the main street and keep to boardwalk. Welshmen, the Cousin Jacks, the Germans, the brawling and the lusty Irish, and the Mexicans from San Luis Potosi all mingled cheek to jowl on its big crowded street.

Faro barkers were pushed to hoarseness by the din from the honky-tonks and saloons, and blooded horses rubbed noses with mules at the tie rails. Mad and rich and profligate as it was, it could get into a man's blood, and it was in Ames's. It was money—raw, brutal and powerful, and he had none of it.

He stepped out into the road to avoid a brawl in front of Harman's Keno Parlor, and a couple of desert rats on the fringe of the curious whooping crowd saw him, waved, and went back to watching the fight.

Ames's Assay Office was a slab affair downstreet past the thick of the saloons. He had a pair of defective scales and some choice pieces of ore as window decorations and that was all.

Beyond the windows was his littered desk and a small third-hand safe bearing the legend on its door, "Seven Seas Whaling Co., San Francisco." He had never had the lettering changed, and it amused him to have people ask how he had come to switch professions.

The safe was backed against a partition, next to some sample bins, and beyond the partition were his tools of trade—retorts, carboys of acid, tables, sample crushers, sieves, molds, and sacks of fuel.

Ames locked the door after him, lighted the lamp, set it on the floor by the safe, and began to fiddle with the safe's dial. There was a report inside which he was to deliver later that evening.

Before he had finished the combination, he heard a knock

on the door, and twisted his head, his hand cupped above the lamp chimney to blow the light.

Then, making sure the safe was still locked, he rose and went over and opened the door. A burly man whose features he could not place, spoke from around a cigar. "Evening, Littlepage. Mind if I come in?"

Ames stepped aside, and the man walked straight on through to the sheltering darkness of the partition. "Let's bring the lamp back here, eh?" His voice had a resonant, slightly false note of geniality.

Ames lifted the lamp from the floor, stepped behind the partition and turned. "Name's Manley," Ames's caller said, holding out a thick-fingered muscled hand. "Know me?"

"Can't say I do," Ames said, shaking hands.

Manley was a big man, almost as tall as Ames himself and thicker because he had gone to fat. Above a rubbery mouth and a small beaked nose his eyes were calculating and utterly without expression, save for a cold brassiness. His clothes were black and unpressed, but the heavy gold watch chain, a solitaire stickpin, and the fine pair of boots, all signs of affluence on the frontier, did not escape Ames.

"Can you spare a few minutes to listen to a proposition, friend?" Manley asked.

"I can't think what it would be, but go ahead." Ames drew out his pipe and packed it, leaning back on a sample bin.

Manley was looking around the room, talking at the same time. "You're doing pretty good here, Littlepage. So-so anyway. Well, that's all right. You got a reputation for absolute honesty in this camp." He turned his head to look at Ames. "Would you sell that reputation for fifty thousand dollars?" he asked in the same casual voice.

Ames scowled. "I don't get it."

"I know. Just think about the fifty thousand dollars a minute. Let me talk." Manley looked at the tip of his cigar.

"You're going to marry Liam Costello's daughter, Cornelia, I've heard. Right?"

Ames said nothing, only watched the man intently.

"No offense meant when I say this, Littlepage, only that takes money. He's rich and you're not."

Ames gave a sudden, sardonic laugh, but Manley's face didn't change. "Suppose you had fifty thousand dollars to invest," Manley said carefully. "Keeping that in mind, let me tell you what I heard today. Costello and Herkenhoff are going to raid Pacific Shares' stock next week. Strictly confidential, you understand. They'll dump their shares until Pacific Shares is quoted at ten. What if you bought five thousand at that price? You'd make money, eh, on Costello's little shenanigan?"

"Make it plain talk, Manley. What are you trying to say?"

"No. Not yet. First, I want to show you that if you made yourself a stake, Liam Costello could triple it for you in a week."

"I know that."

"Sure. Costello's a pirate. He admits it. He's the slickest stock-rigger in this camp."

"What do you want?" Ames asked tolerantly.

Manley laughed and lounged off the table. He started to prowl around the room, talking aimlessly. "Know those two claims north of the Vanity Fair?"

"The Golconda? Sure."

"They're mine," Manley said. His back was to Ames, and he was fingering a pestle. "One hundred and eighty thousand square feet of low-grade gravel, rabbit holes, conglomerate, and scrub cedar. It'll make us both rich."

Ames smiled inwardly at the brass of the man. He knew Manley wanted him to ask questions, and he did.

"Both of us?" he inquired ironically. "But I'm an assayer, not a promoter, Manley."

"Wrong," Manley said, whirling and stabbing a finger at him. "All I need to sell stock in that gravel pit is a favorable assay report, say, eight hundred dollars to the ton in gold and silver. You give it to me and we're rich."

Ames shook his head. "Even a child wouldn't buy mining stock on an assay report."

"Wrong again," Manley said. He strode over to Ames now, and faced him, his voice low and persuasive. "You're likely too modest to notice it, Littlepage, but you've got a mighty fine name with prospectors around here. I don't mean the swindlers and the stockriggers; I mean the bedrock men, the discoverers. They like you. If I can show those old desert rats a good assay from you and prove you've bought some stock in the Golconda, they'll talk. They'll carry the word. Pretty soon, the small suckers, the riffraff, the gamblers, the honky-tonk girls, the Mexes, the freighters, all the small-money stuff, will take a ride on my fifty-dollars-a-share stock. I'll peddle it and duck out with half the loot. The other half is yours."

"Just a cheap swindle," Ames said slowly.

"That's it. Only not so cheap. I figure we can make a hundred thousand on it. And you'll be absolutely safe."

Ames looked at him closely. "How do you figure that? I'll have given a crooked assay on worthless ore."

"Oh, no," Manley said, smiling. "Oh, no. I wouldn't let you in for that. The ore I bring in to you will assay at eight hundred dollars a ton. Of course, that ore won't be from the Golconda, but you'd have had no way of knowing that."

"It doesn't ring true, Manley," Ames remarked shrewdly. "All you had to do to put this swindle across was bring me the ore. As you say, I wouldn't have known where it came from." He paused. "Why are you offering to make money for me when you could have kept it all yourself?"

Manley smiled disarmingly and dropped his cigar and stepped on it. "That's to the point," he murmured. "The reason I'm splitting with you is pretty simple. You marry Liam Costello's girl. He'll put you next to a dozen deals where you can make money. You're on top. All right, when you're there you won't forget me. When you rig up a really big swindle, you cut me in. Plain business. Favor for favor."

He held up a hand. "Don't say anything now. Think it over. And just remember a couple of things: You're protected, you take no risk. And the deal doesn't smell a bit more than Costello's or Herkenhoff's or Mathias's or any of the big boys." He smiled. "I'll send my samples around in the morning. Good night." He went out without shaking hands.

When the front door closed behind Manley, Ames did not move for a moment. He was waiting for the anger and the resentment to come. Somehow it didn't. Manley was a scoundrel, of course, but cynical enough to admit it. Ames laughed, picked up the lamp and went back to the safe.

While Ames was fiddling with the dial, Manley's words kept creeping into the front of his mind. The scheme, of course was a swindle, but no worse than things Costello pulled, as Manley had said.

Suddenly Ames paused in his dialing, stopped by a memory. That Westwind King mine of Liam Costello's that had failed three months ago. On the rumor that a ledge of pure silver sulphurets had been uncovered, Costello had pulled in some big promotion money. For five months the mine had paid well, a dividend was declared, and then the vein disappeared. Or had it? Was the vein ever big enough or deep enough to warrant a huge stock issue?

Stockholders in London and Vienna, where the issues were floated, had gambled on Costello's name and luck. Wasn't it all a swindle, planned and executed in the realms of big money, where bluff, brass, wits, and luck served for sagacity and acumen?

Ames shook his head as if in answer to some inner prompting, got the papers he wanted, closed the safe, and stood up, a small anger and excitement crawling within him. In a few minutes he would be talking and drinking with these big stockriggers, and no guilt would show on their faces. They were good men, sober, generous, shrewd, industrious. And they were nice to him, liked him well enough to throw business his way when they could.

Blowing out the lamp, Ames looked around the dingy office and back room where he and his helper worked, and suddenly he was disgusted with it and a little ashamed. Out on the street he stopped at the nearest saloon for a drink, and then made his way up the crowded street to the Union House.

Ames climbed a spacious flight of stairs to the right of the lobby and paused at the door of Liam Costello's suite. He was admitted to a foyer by a Mexican maid who took his hat, led him through a short corridor where the smell of rich cigars eddied by him, and then into the large drawing room whose windows looked out onto the main street.

Of the half dozen women there, some of them young, Cornelia Costello was easily the most attractive to look at. She had been watching the door and she came over to Ames immediately, her walk so indolent that it barely stirred the full skirts of her flowered yellow silk dress. She was tall and slim and sulky-looking with her dark creamy skin and eyes that were sometimes brown, sometimes violet. Her mouth was arrogant and full of humor, the lips generous and almost pouting. She had a kind of mocking, lazy way about her that could stir Ames to disapproval, then make him laugh with delight.

She kissed him, a little too affectionately for this time and place, and then led him over to the table of whist where the Herkenhoffs, man and wife, the Lowry girl with Wieboldt and his two guests from San Francisco, and Liam Costello were lounging.

Costello, a black Irish, small and with a shrewd, humorous face, was holding up the game long enough to dare bets on the next hand. He shook hands with Ames, quieted long enough to make introductions, and then resumed his jeering. When there were no takers, he excused himself, poured a drink from one of the bottles on the buffet, handed it to Ames, and then took him and Cornelia over to the young woman and two men who were looking out the window at the street below. It was a free and easy kind of gathering, informal, an almost nightly affair but one still exciting to Ames.

"Pity about the cave-in at the Hopeful last night," Costello remarked, looking down on the crowded street. "No mourning out there, though. How many men caught?"

"Seventeen," Ames answered.

"Why don't we turn our party tomorrow night into a benefit for the widows?" Cornelia asked. "It would be fun."

"It would be a brawl, Connie," her father said.

"No. Not that kind of party. We could make a nice german of it down in the lobby and dining room, with tickets at twenty dollars each, the money to go to the fund." Her eyes began to glow with excitement. "Would the hotel let us, dad?"

"They'd better," Costello said cheerfully, "or I'll vacate a floor for them."

"Would you like it, Ames?" Connie asked.

Before Ames could answer, the other girl, a stranger from the coast, said she, too, thought it would be fun. The group moved over to consult the whist players and Costello was left with Ames.

"Harum-scarum," Costello said. His gray-shot hair rode his tight little skull like a stiff brush. He mouthed a cigar with nervous impatience.

"I heard something tonight," Ames said carelessly. "Money talk. I wondered if it were true."

"What was it?"

"That you're going to raid the Pacific Shares bunch next week."

Costello peered up at Ames from under thick black brows, his glance curious, but giving away nothing. "Since when," he asked, "have you been interested in market talk? Going to get in?"

"Maybe."

"Then come to me, like I've invited you. A tip you pick up on the street is put there for a purpose. It's a lie—invariably." He paused, watching the younger man's face with kindly shrewdness. "Ames, I've tried to help you before."

"I've never had the money to start with," Ames said slowly, in a tone whose carelessness surprised even himself.

"You've got it now? How much?"

"Around fifty thousand." The minute he said it Ames knew the decision had been made when he left the office, and he felt a momentary doubt.

"Good. I'll double it in short order. I'll double that, too," Costello said, grinning. He regarded Ames with complete affection. "You're all right, son. You're proud. You wanted to make your stake first, and I don't blame you." He laughed. "For a while, I had you figured as timid."

Cornelia, who had come up to them in time to hear her father's last words, looked amused. "Ames timid?" she drawled. "He'll be a buccaneer after your own cut, dad. You'll see." She smiled up at Ames with lazy friendliness, and Ames took her hand, strangely angry. This was all it took to make him one of them. Suddenly he had to ask a question of Cornelia, and he did, the urgency of it carefully disguised.

"Would you still have married me if I *had* been timid, Connie?"

She looked at him with gentle mockery in her eyes and then squeezed his hand. "Bless you, I was going to, Ames." And then, as if to tease him she added, "But the pirate in you was obvious. I knew it would break through."

"Money," Costello said, "is simply the dividend of guts."

"Put coarsely," his daughter added.

Costello nodded grimly, arrogantly, smiling at her. "Why not? A slaughterhouse is coarse, and nobody denies it. So is making money, only you slaughter a different breed of sheep."

Herkenhoff, a bald man with a cunning expression on his soft, fat face, came over. "We've got enough for a table of poker, Liam," he said impatiently. "It's either that or I'm going to sleep in a chair."

Ames went home at five in the morning, his brain tired and fogged with smoke and liquor. Bare dawn had touched the desert to the east with a momentary coolness, and to the west the clean bare sweep of the Pintwaters was almost cold-looking. The sun was touching the tip of the highest peak when he let himself in.

Out in the kitchen he could hear the muffled clatter of activity. He paused at the stairwell, wondering at this depression, and not allowing himself to think of his decision to take up Manley's proposition.

Suddenly, he turned and walked through the dining room and opened the kitchen door. Lily, waiting for a hot fire, was taking the cloths off the pans of bread which had been set to rise during the night. She looked at Ames and said, "Morning. Going or coming?"

Ames grinned back. "Coming, I guess. No, I'm not. I've got work to do today." He looked around him. "Got any wood to chop?"

"Cords of it."

"Good. It'll clear my head." He tramped through the kitchen, peeling off his coat, and then he paused at the door and rammed his hand in his pocket. He brought out a handful of gold coins and jingled them, his eyes on Lily. She looked fresh and pretty as she came over and regarded the coins in his palm.

"You won," she said, her glance traveling up to his face.

Ames nodded. "I'm on a lucky streak."

"You always have been," Lily told him. "All you needed was to find it out."

Ames was about to speak, and then unaccountably his face flushed. He went out and chopped wood for two hours. Then he ate and went down to work. At nine o'clock two big sacks were dumped in the alley behind the place. They contained the ore from Manley.

By mid-afternoon, Ames found that Manley had guessed

right. The ore assayed at seven hundred dollars the ton—four hundred and fifty dollars in gold, two hundred and fifty dollars in silver. He made out his assay sheet in detail, left it on a spike in the safe for Manley to call for it, and went home and slept.

Like any tight clan, mining folk take care of their own. Scarcely a night passed but what someone, quarreling over a claim, a table stake, a drink, or a girl, was killed. Men stepped over his body to buy a beer, not even trying to remember the face. But let a drift cave in, killing the men who were working in it, and it was different, for there were ways and ways of dying.

When the hat was passed for the widow around the saloons and gambling halls, a gambler would cash in his stack of chips before him, scrape the gold in the hat, and wish the survivors well, not even knowing their names. A honky-tonk girl would contribute a night's earnings. A saloon would raffle a hat at twenty dollars a throw, selling every customer a chance, and turn over the proceeds to the fund. Or, like tonight, a dance at the Union House would be organized, where none was barred and the ticket of admission was twenty dollars. All, from the passed hat to the dance, were peace offerings on the altar of luck, made by a superstitious and open-handed folk.

Lily Donovan, in a blue silk dress that seemed to touch her honey-colored hair with a thousand lights, went to the dance with Phil Michelson, a young engineer from the Union Consolidated.

Sweet charity was smiling so brightly that the Sage Hen, rotund duenna of twenty honky-tonk girls, shook hands with Connie, smiled modestly at Ames, and comported herself with the dignity of a duchess. The men of that woman-hungry camp were scrubbed and polished and sober enough to keep within the strict bounds of decorum. Whoever did not was ushered out swiftly by bouncers loaned from a half dozen saloons. It was gay and fun, completely democratic, perhaps because death, in whose honor it was really held, set the example.

Connie, in a white, low-necked dress, was besieged from the start by all the young and personable men in the camp. Ames watched her billowing white skirt on the floor, and smiled with pride. When she passed him, her face flushed with excitement, she would wiggle her fingers in a little salute. After her partner returned her to Ames, following one dance, she said breathlessly, "Who are all these men? They're so nice and all good dancers."

"The broke and ambitious," Ames said, aware of his own membership in their class.

"I'm tired," Connie complained taking his arm. "Who has the next dance with me?"

"Phil Michelson."

"I don't know him," Connie said carelessly. "Let's go up to the suite for some punch."

"Can't," Ames said shortly. "It's a contract."

Connie looked briefly at him. "Point him out to me."

Ames spotted Phil and Lily across the room, talking to Big Joe Hyde, a saloon owner, and his wife.

"He doesn't look interesting," Connie said when Ames pointed to Phil. "Let's go up."

"But Connie, I promised."

Connie searched his face. His obstinacy seemed to touch a spark of resentment in her. "But, darling, I don't want to. I'm tired. Will you come along?"

"He's a nice fellow," Ames said humbly. "I live with him."

"But you live in a boarding house, Ames. Do I have to dance with everyone in the boarding house? Now come along."

"I'll take you to the stairs, but I'm coming back," Ames said stubbornly.

Connie's face changed imperceptibly as she understood the implication. "Oh, you'd like to stay and dance with his partner?"

"Yes. It's custom, isn't it?"

"Who is she?"

"Lily Donovan. She runs the boardinghouse with her mother. She's my good friend, Connie," Ames explained.

"I'll stay, of course," Connie yielded immediately, humbly, just as the fiddles swung into a schottische.

Phil and Lily came over, and the introductions were made. Connie smiled pleasantly at Lily, who regarded her with friendly, unimpressed eyes, and then the two couples separated to dance.

"She's very lovely, Ames," Lily said. "You don't have to tell me you think that, too, so don't say anything."

"Ames laughed softly, his arm around Lily. One of the things about Lily was her understanding of how a man felt, her straightforwardness. He found himself comparing it with Connie's femininity, and then, afraid that he was being disloyal, he put it from his mind.

Connie and Phil met them at the end of the dance, and Ames saw that Phil looked harassed and uncomfortable, while Connie's face was bland and proud. She put her arm in Ames' as soon as he joined her. Lily murmured something about the crowd.

"Tell me, Miss Donovan," Connie said curiously, "aren't you the girl that runs Ames's boardinghouse?"

"Yes," Lily answered easily.

"Isn't it hard?"

Lily smiled. "It's work," she admitted.

"Do you make much money at it?"

Lily was still smiling, and Ames looked down quickly at Connie. Lily laughed, "I had over eight hundred dollars in the bank this morning. A year's work."

"Really?" Connie said, genuinely surprised. "Why, I pay my maid more than that. Perhaps I could put you in touch with some of my friends who could place you in service."

For a moment Lily did not speak, and Ames could see the amazement and hurt well up in her eyes. He looked at Connie, almost ready to express his anger, and what he saw baffled him. Connie, too, had observed the hurt in Lily's face, and she was honestly distressed and bewildered. She glanced up at Ames, pleading for help and an explanation. What was wrong?—her eyes seemed to ask.

But Connie had tact, and she said no more. She put out her hand and Lily took it. "It was nice to meet you both," Connie said sincerely. "I have a headache. I think I'll go upstairs." She shook hands with Phil Michelson.

Ames, as he left, pressed Lily's arm, and then turned away, Connie on his arm.

They went through the lobby and upstairs, not speaking, but when they were in the drawing room, Connie turned to Ames. "What did I say down there that hurt her, Ames? What did I do?"

"You don't understand?" Ames asked wonderingly.

"Do you think I would hurt a girl intentionally? Your friend? And I hurt her. What did I say?"

"You offered to get her a place as a servant with your friends, Connie."

"Shouldn't I have done that? I only meant to be kind, to help her." Connie's eyes were pleading for understanding and forgiveness, and Ames felt his anger drain away. There was nothing he could say, no way to explain the gulf that lay between them, but he was determined to try.

"Sit down, Connie." She sat in a deep chair and Ames stood before her, his brow wrinkled in a frown.

"Lily and her mother own that boardinghouse. Donovan was a mine super, killed in an accident like this cave-in at the Hopeful. Lily and her mother were left with a little stake, and they turned it into this boardinghouse. They're making out, all right, even saving a little money."

His voice trailed off in hopelessness. Connie was listening intently, and heard every word, and yet there was no understanding in her eyes, her face, her attitude.

"But she works hard," Connie said. "I only had to look at her hands. She's attractive, and Judy Herkenhoff would love her for a maid. Wouldn't it be better than taking in boarders? Wouldn't she make more money?"

Ames smiled ruefully, and said nothing. Connie leaned back and covered her face with her hands. "I'm so sorry. But I can't understand what I've done, Ames."

"You're tired," Ames said. "Maybe you ought to get some sleep."

She agreed and Ames kissed her good night and went downstairs, his step deliberate, his eyes musing. Lily and Phil were not in the hall. He got a drink at Harman's and went back to Donovan's.

The dining room was dark, and he tiptoed through it to the kitchen. There was no light there, and no light on the porch. He wanted to talk to Lily, to explain it all to her, tell her that Connie had not meant to hurt her.

But could he tell her that Connie had so little understanding that she could see no hurt in what she had said? Could he make Lily believe that money, the amount of it a person had, was all that counted with Connie? Either you didn't have it or you did. All the people who did have it, or were going to get it, like himself, were her equals; those who did not have it, should try and get it and were all one class, her inferiors, like her servants.

When Ames went down to get his shaving water before breakfast next morning, Lily was in the kitchen.

"Lily," he began, "about Connie last night."

"Let's not talk about it," said Lily. "I'd rather not."

"Let's do," Ames said grimly.

Lily glanced at him briefly. "You want to apologize for the woman you're going to marry, Ames. That's not right, and you know it. Why should you?"

"She didn't mean to hurt you."

"I really believe she didn't mean to, Ames. Can't we let it go at that?"

Ames reached out and turned Lily to face him, and then

let his hands drop from her shoulders. "I asked her afterward," he said, his glance steady on Lily's face. "She said she really wanted to help you." His eyes suddenly avoided hers. "It's Costello's money," he murmured, with a bitterness he could not keep out of his voice. "It's built a wall around him and Connie and their friends. Everyone who can climb that wall is welcome. Then they ask the stranger about the people outside—like Connie asked you last night."

Lily laughed suddenly, a calm, easy laugh that dissolved some of the tightness in Ames's chest. "But why be so earnest about it, Ames? It's you I know and like."

"But I wanted you to like her."

Lily looked at him keenly and then smiled her secret, wise smile. "That never happens. Maybe it was never meant to happen."

Ames understood that, and he nodded, but he was dissatisfied. Lily was wise, and knew instinctively the things of which a man was ignorant or which he was too stubborn to recognize. He was the one who had been anxious for Lily to meet Connie. Lily had never moved to meet her. Even last night, it was he who arranged the exchange of dances, not Lily, not Phil. And yet, it could have turned out differently, and he voiced this thought. "When I've married and made some money and lost it, Lily," he said with wry humor, "you and Connie will be friends."

"Or when I've made myself rich, like I'm going to," Lily said lightly.

Ames grinned. "You've decided to be rich, not a servant?"

Lily looked at him and laughed and it was all right again. He put a leg on the table and sat down. "Yes, I decided yesterday, Ames," Lily said. "Or rather, Phil did for me. We're going to be rich."

"Married?" Ames asked, his pulse quickening.

Lily made a grimace of mock horror. "Certainly not. It's a friendly pool to make a million—and avoid the life of a lady's maid."

"How do you go about this?" Ames asked, strangely relieved.

Lily shrugged and raised her eyebrows. "You give a man money, and he gives you a piece of paper. Pretty soon, he comes and tells you that other people want to buy your paper, and you sell it for ten times what you paid for it." She laughed, "It's really very simple."

"Mining stocks, eh? Whose?"

"The Golconda. It's promoted by a man named Manley."

Ames lunged off the table and grabbed Lily by the shoulders and shook her. "Lily, you didn't buy stock!"

"Why . . . why, Ames, what's the matter? Yes. Eight hundred dollars."

Slowly, Ames's arms fell to his side, and he stared at the floor.

"What is it, Ames?" Lily demanded.

"It's a fraudulent stock," Ames said hoarsely.

"But you made the assay on their ore. And you're a stockholder. I saw it."

Ames looked up at her, his eyes tortured and miserable. "Yes. That's how I was going to get rich, Lily," he said bleakly. For one brief instant he saw the pity in her eyes, and then he tramped out of the kitchen. Upstairs he got his hat and coat and came down and went out, turning toward town.

After trying five saloons, he found Manley in the dining room of the Union House at a late breakfast. A few other people were scattered around the room at tables. Ames's face had settled into a tight, pale hardness. He paused by Manley's chair, and without returning the promoter's greeting, asked, "How much money have you taken in, Manley?"

"Why?" Manley looked shrewdly at Ames, unable to gauge his face, and his eyes were suddenly crafty. "Why?" he repeated.

"How much?"

"Six, eight thousand."

"I'd like to see it," Ames said quietly. "I'd like to see the list of buyers, too. Come along. Have you got an office?"

"Yes. Wait until I finish my breakfast."

"Come along," Ames said distinctly.

Manley rose, and Ames followed him out to the street, down it, up an open stairway to a room above a hardware store. The promoter opened a door on whose glass was painted GOLCONDA MINING CO., INC. Beyond it was a spacious room, holding some easy chairs, a table, a desk, and a safe. Manley turned to Ames as soon as the door was locked.

"Has somebody been talking about me?"

"Yes."

"Every dollar I've taken is in that safe!" Manley said hotly.

"Open it and let's see."

Manley went over to it, was silent a moment as he fiddled with the dial, and then swung the door open and stood up. "Count it for yourself."

Ames walked to the stair doorway, unlocked it and opened it and then came back into the middle of the room. "Manley, you're through," he said in a voice edged with controlled anger. "There's a stage leaves at noon for Frisco. Take it."

For a long moment Manley stared at him, puzzled, suspicious. "What for?" he asked softly.

"At noon I'll announce this deal is a fraud and return the money. If you love your hide, clear out!"

It didn't take Manley long to decide. His hand streaked for the gun at his hip. Ames hit him in the face, and Manley crashed against the desk and went down. His gun fell to the floor, and he made a grab for it. Ames kicked it under the safe.

"Get up," Ames said in a choked voice.

Slowly Manley came to his knees, then lunged. Ames straightened him up with an uppercut, then drove a fist into his fat midriff, looped a right over and knocked him down again. Manley staggered to his feet, picked up a chair and threw it.

Ames ducked, then dived at him, and they both went down. From there on it was a wicked fight, with no science, little skill, and all savage anger. They tipped the table end over end, and Ames was knocked back against it. He met Manley's rush with his feet and then shoved.

Manley slammed back against the wall with such violence that a window sash fell down with a crash like the report of a gun. Ames was on him, then, and drove a fist at his shelving jaw, another at his chest, a third at his head. Manley tried vainly to kick, but he was dazed. Ames measured him, feinted with a right aimed at his mid-section, and when Manley's guard dropped, looped over a left with a slap of knuckled studded bone on flesh. Manley went down, tried to rise, and rolled over on his back. Ames dragged him to the door and threw him down the stairs.

Afterward, Ames leaned both arms on the desk, gagging for breath. Then he went over to the safe and cleaned it of sacks of coin, a few notes, and all the papers it contained.

Manley was gone when he went downstairs. Ames hesitated there, weaving with weariness, and then cut across to the Union House and mounted the stairs to Costello's suite.

It was only when the maid gasped as she opened the door, that Ames realized that he was bleeding, his coat ripped, his face bruised and thick-lipped. He brushed past her and into the drawing room, where Connie and Costello were sitting.

"Ames!" Connie cried. She ran over to him, but he did not look at her.

"I've come to turn down your offer to make me some money, Costello," he announced heavily.

Costello was motionless in his chair. "Why?" he asked presently.

"I haven't any. I was going in with Manley on a fake mine. No ore, faked assay, and worthless stock."

"That was clumsy," Costello said wryly. "Do it better next time."

"There won't be any next time," Ames said, looking at

Connie. Her eyes were wide, troubled, unsure. "Connie, I'm a poor man. Maybe I won't always be, but an assayer doesn't make much."

Connie smiled faintly. "You won't always be an assayer, Ames."

"But if I am?"

Connie only shook her head. "You won't, Ames. You'll make a fortune some day. You stumbled this time. You won't next."

That was all he wanted to know. He looked at the sacks of coins in his hands, then glanced up at Costello, and then at her.

"Connie, you offered to marry me once if I let your dad help me. I wouldn't do it. I never will, not the way he means and you mean. Will you still marry me?"

"You're too proud, Ames!" Connie cried. "It's absurd!"

"Will you still marry me?" His voice, his eyes, his manner was relentless.

"Ames, be reasonable!" Connie pleaded. "Don't be so hard, so angry!"

Ames regarded her a moment longer, and then nodded his head, as if agreeing with something. "That's all we've got to say to each other, I reckon. Good-by." He turned and started out.

"Ames!" Connie called imperiously.

He did not even hear her. He let himself out and walked downstreet to the assay office, a curious feeling of happiness within him that he did not recognize as relief.

George, his helper, was working back in the shop. Ames peeled off his coat, sat at his desk, and spent the rest of the morning counting out money, apportioning it according to the names of the stockholders on the sheet.

It was noon when Lily found him thus. Ames rose at her entrance and Lily's breath quickened as she looked at him. "Ames, what have they done to you?"

Ames picked up her money and Phil's, put it in a sack and

handed it to her. "Put it in the bank, Lily. And don't forgive me. I don't deserve it."

At that moment a rock crashed through the window, and the glass shattered, collapsing in a jangle on the floor. Ames swiveled his head to look on the street. In one brief glance he took it in and understood.

The ore wagons, whose unbroken line was seldom interrupted by anything, had been pulled to a halt leaving a wide space between them. Across the street, people were hurrying for shelter. In front of the office the loafers had cleared out.

Manley, his face still bloody, his legs straddled to support him, stood alone in the dust of the street. He had a gun in his left hand. The hot desert sun beat down on him, casting a small pool of black shadow in the white dust at his feet.

"Come out of there, Littlepage!" Manley called.

Ames looked at Lily and then went over to the safe and brought out a gun.

"Get behind the partition, Lily," Ames said quietly.

"Do you have to go?" Lily asked, her voice just as still and restrained as his.

Ames nodded. "I've dodged my medicine long enough."

Lily started for the partition, paused, and came back. She stood on tiptoe and kissed Ames's mouth. "I never wanted you to know. I don't care now," she said. She backed toward the partition, her eyes grave, her face troubled and lovely.

"That's the way it was meant to be all along, Lily," Ames told her huskily. He turned and walked out onto the step, the gun in his hand.

"The stage has gone," Manley taunted. "Here I am."

"Make your talk, Manley," Ames said quietly.

"I want to see you beg," sneered the promoter. "Like you begged your way to Costello's girl. Like you begged for money. Beg—because you're a gone goose, Littlepage."

"I'm through begging," Ames said simply.

Manley began to curse him then, calling him names that make men fight. Ames's face was a pale mask.

"Manley, you're a cheap crook. A tinhorn stock promoter.

So was I. I'm not now." He watched Manley carefully. "I'm coming out there now and beat you again."

Manley laughed wildly and swung up his gun to shoulder level. He brought it down like a club in a swift, wild urgency, and shot, the noise hammering in the street.

Ames raised his gun slowly, as Manley shot again, stirring the dust under the boardwalk. When the white of Manley's shirt lay between the notch of his back sight, and the front sight appeared in a slow lift, Ames fired once and then lowered his arm.

Manley shot again into the dust, moving a leg to support himself. Then his gun arm fell. He tried to say something and could not. He raised a hand to his chest and his left knee buckled. He fell, kneeling, and then pitched gently into the dust.

Ames turned and walked into the office. Lily had come out from behind the partition.

"I've been crooked, Lily," Ames said. "Rotten crooked."

"I know. And foolish," Lily whispered. "Mostly foolish. But, darling, you aren't now! You never were, really!"

"But not again," Ames said, and his arms closed around her tightly, hungrily.

LAWYER TWO-FIST

Wayne D. Overholser

STORIES about frontier lawyers were not uncommon in the Western pulps, as "Lawyer Two-Fist"—and the much different tale by Dan Cushman which you'll find later in these pages— attest. The Old West was an unruly and untamed country in the 1860s and 1870s. Sheriffs and marshals could only do so much to keep the peace; it was up to the pioneer lawyers and judges to see that the law was upheld and the balance of justice carried out. These "legal eagles" were all too often forced to use fists and guns to supplement their courtroom efforts; but even for a tough "Lawyer Two-Fist," the most satisfying victory was the one brought about by guile and a little honest deceit.

Wayne D. Overholser published his first short story in Popular Western *in 1936, and followed it with several hundred more in such well-known—and such obscure—pulps as* Western Story, Romance Roundup, Wild West Weekly, Texas Rangers, Rio Kid Western, *and* Rodeo Romances. *His first novel,* Buckaroo's Code, *appeared in 1947; of the 99 subsequent titles penned over the ensuing thirty-five years, two were recipients of Western Writers of America Spur Awards as the best novels of their respective years—*The Lawman, *as by Lee Leighton, in 1953, and* The Violent Land *in 1954. Novel number 100,* Danger Trail, *appeared in 1982. His most recent book is a long overdue collection,* The Best Western Stories of Wayne D. Overholser *(1984).*

It was spring in Gunsmoke Basin, spring with the snow but a week gone. Along the sidewalks of Trailsend the swollen cottonwood buds bore promise of a rapidly approaching

73

summer, a promise of growth and warmth that found no echo in the heart of Frank Mort.

A grim hardness was in Mort's eyes as he knocked the dottle out of his pipe and looked across the counter at his friend, Slim Harper.

"If we could beat Lengel at something," he said, "not much, but just anything, we'd bust him wide open. All we got to do is to prove to the ranchers that Lengel's not as smart and tough as he thinks."

"Reckon so," Slim nodded, "but beating Lengel at anything is just what hasn't been done since he sloped into the Basin."

"I haven't had much of a crack at it," Mort said softly, "seeing as I've just been back in town a couple of months."

Nobody would ever have shot Frank Mort for a lawyer just on looks. A bronzed lathe of a man, this Frank Mort, with whiplash muscles and a pinched-in-the-middle appearance that was mute evidence of years spent in the saddle. Yet for all his cowman appearance, he was a lawyer and a good one.

He could have gone to the state capital and made ten times the money he could ever hope to make in the sleepy little cow town of Trailsend, but this was home. Here he had spent all his life until he had gone away to law school. He'd left it a happy town; he'd returned to find it sullen, fear-stricken. The difference lay in one Hard Cash Lengel.

The year Mort had left Trailsend to go to law school, Lengel had bought the Rafter 9, and the combination of hired gun slicks, money, and a drought had made him ruler of the Basin. When the drought came the ranchers needed money. Lengel had it and loaned it.

"The first thing I saw," Mort said thoughtfully as he stuffed the bowl of his pipe, "was the way folks around here bow to Lengel. There's a few that's got guts enough to tell Lengel to go square to hell, including you, Slim, but most of 'em are a bunch of rabbits."

"Yeah, I told him," Slim nodded gloomily at his nearly

empty shelves, "and I lost about nine-tenths of my business. Lengel's mean, Frank. He and that smart talking lawyer of his, Shane, make a tough team. You'll have to figure Shane in on any game you buck Lengel on."

Mort blew out a cloud of smoke and grinned. "I'm figuring on that, too, Slim. I'll get 'em both—"

Pandemonium broke out in the street in front of Harper's store. Someone let out a screech of fright. A bass voice ripped out a string of blistering oaths, and loose boards rattled as men ran along the sidewalk. Mort got up and stared out of the window.

"It's Lengel," he roared. "Talk about the devil and he's bound to appear. He's sure on the prod. Looks like he's about to work somebody over."

Mort stuck his pipe into his pocket and ran out into the street. Lengel was bent over a cowering man, shaking his fist under the other's nose and roaring at the top of his bull fiddle voice.

"You low-down son of a mangy sheepherder," he bellowed, "steal my horse, will you? I'll have you stuck in the calaboose so long you'll never get out."

"I bought him," the little man gasped as he backed away.

"Where's your bill of sale if you bought him?" Lengel thundered.

"I ain't got one."

"You're damned right you ain't. Anybody can see that Rafter 9 brand. You think I'm blind?"

"Is that the horse they're squabbling about?" Mort asked a grinning bystander.

The man nodded. If it hadn't been Lengel, the whole thing would have been laughable. The horse was standing at the hitching rack, his head down, placidly unaware of all the furor. He was a shaggy, swaybacked nag that wasn't good for anything but coyote bait. Lengel wouldn't have had such a horse on his ranch if it had been his. He must have been well past ripe old age, and he was covered with an array of brands that showed he'd been owned by about every ranch between Gunsmoke Basin and the border. There was something behind this that for the moment Mort didn't see, but whatever it was, he aimed to find out.

"I bought him," the little man kept repeating.

"You stole him, Paxson, you damned horse thief." Lengel shouted. "Go git the sheriff, Rip. This sod-buster's gonna get his for stealing my—" He hesitated as if not wanting to insult the entire horse kingdom by calling this animal by that name.

"You mean skate, Lengel," Mort said as he pushed through the circle of men to where Lengel and Paxson were standing. "That bag of bones isn't good for anything but the glue factory, which same I don't need to tell you."

Lengel was so taken aback that for a second he couldn't speak. His avaricious face turned a dull red, then words came in a thundering torrent.

"You been in Trailsend long enough to know folks around here don't talk to me that way. I'm giving you a chance to apologize."

"I'm not taking that chance, Lengel. I'm saying here and now that you're a two-bit chiseler, picking on a little gent who hasn't got much of any way to fight back."

Mort sensed the tightening in the ring around him, sensed the sudden surge of interest. These men feared and hated Lengel. Their sympathies rode with this young lawyer who had the temerity to call the boss of Gunsmoke Basin, yet he could expect no help.

"You got a slick tongue, lawyer, but that ain't helping you now. I'm gonna take you apart and feed you to the coyotes. I'm gonna—" Still talking, his huge right fist leaped out in a clublike blow that would have knocked Mort cold.

The blow whizzed over Mort's head for he knew the nature of the man in front of him and he'd expected the sudden attack. He ducked, came up under Lengel's right, and both his own fists went out in a paralyzing one-two to Lengel's jaw that rocked the big man to his heels. Mort ducked another swinging uppercut and came in again, his fists driving with pistonlike precision into Lengel's middle. Lengel's breath went out in a wheezing gurgle and he went down into the dust of the street.

A spontaneous cheer went up from the crowd to die suddenly as they realized they'd unwisely given way to their real feelings.

"What's going on here?" A man elbowed into the center of the ring and stopped in surprise as he saw Lengel groggily getting to his feet. It was Sam Ruble, the sheriff. "Stop it," he bellowed when he saw Lengel was starting for Mort again. "We don't allow any brawling in the streets. I heard you wanted me, Mr. Lengel."

Lengel glared at Mort, and the lawyer had never seen so much murderous hatred in a man's eyes.

"I'll settle with you later," he grated, and to the sheriff, "I want Dave Paxson arrested for stealing that horse."

"You mean that . . . that—"

"That's what I said," Lengel snapped. "You can see that Rafter 9 brand, can't you?"

"Sure, sure," Ruble nodded. "Come along, Paxson."

"I bought the horse," the little man protested.

"He ain't got a bill of sale," Lengel said.

"That right?" Ruble asked.

"I ain't got the bill of sale, but I bought him right enough. I paid ten dollars for him."

The crowd tittered, and someone yelled out, "You got cheated, Paxson."

"Come on," the sheriff said impatiently. "You can tell the judge about buying him."

Mort stepped up on the sidewalk and grinned at Slim Harper.

"Too bad the sheriff stopped that," he said.

"Yeah," Slim nodded, "it did me a lot of good the way you smacked him around, but I wish you hadn't. You got yourself into a nice jackpot of trouble. If I was you, I'd kinda make myself scarce for a while."

"Nope," Mort shook his head, "I'm going to take on a law case."

"Stay out of it, Frank. You've done more'n enough already."

"Thanks, Slim. See you later."

"You ain't got a chance with—"

Mort walked away, leaving Slim talking. Ruble was in his office when Mort got there.

"I oughta lock you up, Frank," the sheriff said angrily. "Lengel runs this town. You know that."

"I know he's not going to railroad little Paxson if I can help it. I figure this might be the chance I need to show him and that slick Shane up. I want to talk to Paxson, Sam."

Ruble shrugged his shoulders. "Some gents just can't learn. Go ahead. He's in the third cell."

Mort walked down the corridor until he found Paxson. The little man was sitting on the cot, looking disconsolately out of the barred window.

"Paxson, I'm going to be your lawyer," Mort said. "I want to know who you bought that nag from?"

"It's no use, Mr. Mort," Paxson said hopelessly,. "He's been deviling me for a year. He'll send me to the pen sure."

"Maybe not. Go ahead and tell me where you got the horse."

"Bought him from old man Slaughter last fall. A bunch of Rafter 9 horses drifted across the summit during the summer onto Slaughter's Running W spread. Lengel didn't need 'em, so he sold the bunch to Slaughter. That old skate was in the bunch. Dunno how Lengel ever got him."

"He hasn't got a Running W brand," Mort pointed out.

"Yeah," Paxson nodded. "Slaughter hadn't got around to

branding 'em yet. I never thought anybody'd claim him, so I never got a bill of sale."

"You say Lengel's been deviling you. What about?"

"He wants the one hundred and sixty acres I homesteaded. Offered me fifty dollars to sell. He knows if I don't get my crop in, I'll lose out. Without old Buster I can't do no plowing, and I ain't got a nickel to buy another horse."

Mort nodded. "Simple enough. Your homestead lies between the Rafter 9 and Widow Sims's Quarter Circle 20, doesn't it?"

"Yeah, but what am I gonna do?"

"Sit here," Mort grinned. "I kinda think I can throw Mr. Lengel and hogtie him. Judge Barnes is holding court here day after tomorrow. You're going to stand trial. Then we'll see what we can see. So long, Paxson."

Mort went out whistling and walked down to the livery stable to take another look at the horse.

"Funny anybody'd raise a hooraw about that old skate, isn't it?" he asked Ben Neff, the liveryman.

Neff moved his toothless jaws over his quid and gazed at the horse disapprovingly.

"It is that, Frank," he nodded. "I'm ashamed to have him in here."

Mort moved to the back of the barn to where a gate separated the stalls from the grain bins.

"Looks like you got quite a shipment of grain in," Mort observed, nodding at a pile of filled sacks.

"Yeah," Neff placidly moved his jaws, "a hundred bushel of oats and some wheat for Widder Jenkins's chickens. I'll haul it out to her the last of the week."

Mort shrugged and turned back to the horse stalls.

"Saddle me a good bronc, Ben," he ordered. "I'm riding over to see Buck Slaughter."

As Mort jogged along over the road that led to Slaughter's Running W, he knew that the success of his whole case depended upon the oldster's willingness to testify, and Mort felt reasonably sure he would. Slaughter was made of different stuff than most of the Basin ranchers, and he had no particular love for Lengel.

Mort was not disappointed in Slaughter's answer.

"Sure," the old man said after Mort had outlined the case, "I remember Paxson buying that crowbait. So," he pursed out his plump little cheeks, "Hard Cash Lengel is trying to railroad Paxson. You can bet your bottom dollar I'll be in town day after tomorrow and say a few things that'll burn Lengel's ears. I don't go much on nesters, but Paxson can't ride no more and I owe him a lift. He's having a hard enough time making a go of things."

"It isn't so much that Lengel actually has all these ranchers over a barrel financially," Mort said, "it's mostly a proposition of showing Lengel up as a tinhorn and puncturing his little balloon of success. A lot of the boys just kinda like to ride along with the gent that's winning. And say, hole up in a room until we need you. If Lengel sees you, he'll know why you're in town."

Slaughter nodded, "I'll keep out of sight. In my opinion, Lengel ain't much of an addition to the Basin, him and that lawyer Shane."

So as Mort rode back to Trailsend, he knew it wasn't just enough to prove that Paxson actually owned the horse. Lengel had to be shown up, had to be made the laughingstock before the community. Mort thought of one thing after another, but nothing seemed quite good enough, not until he was turning his mount over to Ben Neff. Then he got an idea that would turn the trick if it worked.

He was in his office in the middle of the afternoon when Shane came in. Shane was one man Mort couldn't stand, a hatchet-faced gent with an oily tongue that made folks give him a confidence he didn't deserve. Because he was Lengel's man, he got the law business of Trailsend.

Shane stood in the doorway a minute, stroking his closely cropped mustache and letting his beady eyes play over Mort's face. Then he said, "I hear you're representing Paxson tomorrow."

"That's right," Mort nodded, and restrained an impulse to throw him out.

"You better change your mind, Mort," Shane purred. "Nobody bucks Lengel in this town. It'd be healthier if you'd mosey on before court opens tomorrow. If you don't, something's liable to happen." There was no mistaking the menace in his tone.

"Reckon I'll stay," Mort answered.

Shane shrugged his shoulders. "I warned you," he said as he stepped back and walked down the street.

Violent anger burned through Mort's veins as he watched Shane disappear into the Gem Saloon. So they thought they could scare him! Well, there were some things even smart jaspers like Lengel and Shane didn't know, and Mort had a hunch they didn't savvy Judge Barnes. The judge was an old-timer in the state, had been circuit judge here for ten years. Maybe he didn't know much law, but he was a product of the cattle country, and he had a great sense of human justice. Lengel had won every case he'd brought up since Mort had been back in Trailsend, but there had never been anybody to testify against him.

It was afternoon the next day before Paxson's case came up. Only a few minutes were needed to call the jury. They were all small ranchers in the Basin, men who feared Lengel, but like most of the others had no reason to love him.

Lengel was suing to recover his horse. If he won, Paxson would later be tried for horse stealing, and if Lengel proved the horse was his, there wasn't much Paxson could do but plead guilty. Mort was aware of that, but he seemed unperturbed as he listened to Lengel's case.

It was evening before Shane was finished. He didn't

present anything new. Lengel swore the horse was his, a half dozen witnesses testified that the horse wore the Rafter 9 brand, and Paxson admitted he had no bill of sale.

When Shane was done, Judge Barnes cleared his throat and looked at Lengel from under his bushy brows.

"Mr. Lengel," he said, "the witnesses have all testified that this horse carries at least fifteen other brands besides the Rafter 9. Are you sure it is yours?"

Lengel stood up.

"Of course it's my horse," he snapped. "None of them other brands represent ranches within two hundred miles of here."

"Apparently it is a very old horse," the judge continued. "I'd like to know what valuation you set upon the animal."

A titter ran around the courtroom and the judge pounded his gavel. Lengel bit his lips and looked at Shane. Then he said, "I don't know how old the horse is, but I haven't had him for some time. Looks like Paxson hid him out all winter. Since I've been without his service all this time, I'd say the horse is worth about five hundred dollars."

The titter rose to a guffaw and died as the judge pounded for order.

"Court dismissed for tonight," he said.

Mort crossed the street to the hotel. Slaughter was in his room where he had stayed all afternoon.

"It went just like I figured," Mort told the old man, "We'll have our crack at it first thing in the morning. You keep out of sight until then."

"Sure," Slaughter grinned, "I want to see Lengel's face when you call me up."

Events moved fast and hard the next morning just as Mort planned. He called Paxson to the stand first. The nester claimed he'd bought the horse, and for the first time he named the seller. Just as the name of Buck Slaughter passed his lips, the street door of the courtroom opened and a man came in. An audible gasp swept the courtroom, for the newcomer was the man Paxson had just named.

"Buck Slaughter to the stand," Mort said, and when the oath had been administered, he asked, "Have you seen the horse that is being held by Ben Neff in the livery stable, claimed by both the defendant and the plaintiff?"

Slaughter nodded his shaggy head. "Sure have, Mr. Mort."

"Did you recognize the horse?"

"Sure. I couldn't mistake that bunch of bones. Hard Cash Lengel ran him in with a bunch of broncs I bought from him last fall."

"What did you do with the horse?"

"He wasn't hardly worth slapping a brand on. Reckon I'd 'a' shot him and put him out of his misery if Paxson hadn't showed up and wanted a farm horse. I sold it to him for ten dollars."

Mort turned to the judge, "The defense rests," he said, and sat down. He grinned as he glanced sideways at Lengel and Shane. Both men were staring pop-eyed at Slaughter as the old man took his seat in the audience. The impossible had happened. For the first time since Hard Cash Lengel had risen to power in Gunsmoke Basin a man had dared testify against him.

The foreman of the jury was standing up.

"We don't need to go out, your honor," he was saying. "We find the animal belongs to Paxson."

Lengel and Shane were on their feet, glaring at each other.

"You lamebrained son of a flea-eaten sheepherder," Lengel shouted, "why didn't you keep Slaughter out of here?"

"I didn't know he was in town," Shane flared back. "I'm not taking that kind of talk from a crooked—"

Then Lengel hit him, and Shane sprawled back into the laps of two women sitting in the front row.

The judge was pounding with his gavel and yelling for order, but order wasn't restored until Sheriff Ruble jerked

Lengel into a chair and shoved a gun into his middle. Shane got to his feet and sneaked out.

"You're fined one hundred dollars for contempt of court." Judge Barnes glared at Lengel.

"Your honor," Mort shouted above the confusion, "this case isn't settled yet. My client has been the victim of a conspiracy on the part of Hard Cash Lengel. Lengel has been bothering him for a year, finally going to the length of having him arrested on the charge which has been proven false."

"Hold on, Mr. Mort," the judge broke in. "There are some features about this case that haven't been made clear to me. Sam," he addressed the bailiff, "tell Ben Neff to bring that horse around to the courthouse. I want to see him."

Five minutes later Neff came in looking very unhappy.

"Is the horse in front, Ben?" the judge asked.

"Well, no." Neff's face grew very red and he looked down at the floor. "You see, the critter's dead. He got loose last night and ate a mess of wheat. I had it stored in the back for Widder Jenkins. I don't know how he did it, judge. Nothing like that ever happened before."

The courtroom was absolutely still for the greater part of a minute. Then the judge said, "Mr. Lengel, it has been proved that the charge against Mr. Paxson is false, and the jury decided the horse belonged to Mr. Paxson, a fact which you well knew. It was because of you that the horse was held in the livery stable, a fact which led to his death. You stated that the horse was worth five hundred dollars. The court orders you to pay Mr. Paxson that five hundred dollars and costs."

Lengel sputtered and started to swear. Just then the audience began to comprehend what had happened. Roars of laughter swept the courtroom, feet stomped and somebody yelled, "Five hundred dollars for that pile of bones!"

Lengel paid and marched out of the courtroom to the hoots and howls of the crowd. They folowed him outside, chanting, "Five hundred dollars, five hundred dollars."

Paxson looked at the roll of bills the judge gave him as if he couldn't believe what had happened. Then he grabbed Mort's hand.

"I was all ready to go to the pen," he grinned. "I dunno how to thank you. Here"—he pressed the bills into Mort's hand—"take 'em."

"No thanks." Mort shoved the bills into Paxson's shirt pocket. "I got pay enough, just getting the best of Lengel. Go buy yourself a real horse and fix your homestead up. Come on, Slim," he said to Harper, "let's see the rest of this."

Outside, Lengel had climbed into his saddle and was galloping out of town. The crowd was in the middle of the street, still yelling, "Five hundred dollars for a pile of bones!"

"You know, Frank," Slim Harper said as they walked toward his store, "you just about fixed Lengel. He won't be counting for much around here now, what with the licking you gave him the other day and then getting the best of him today. Reckon Shane'll pull out, too, and you're just about fixed up in the law business."

"Yeah, I feel pretty good," Mort grinned as he started to fill his pipe.

"There's one thing about this horse I'd like to know," Slim stated, glancing sideways at Mort. "I was in the livery barn this morning just before court took up, and that skate was sure dead. Ben was going around in circles. He couldn't understand it. Said a horse had never got loose in his barn before, let alone open that gate and get into the grain. I took a look at the rope that had been tied to his halter, and it looked to me like maybe it'd been cut. I don't suppose you'd know about that, would you, Frank, or how that gate happened to be open?"

Mort lighted his pipe and grinned at Harper through a cloud of blue smoke.

"Now wouldn't you like to know, Slim," he said.

ENOUGH GOLD

W. Ryerson Johnson

"NORTHERNS"—stories set in the rough-and-tumble frontier days of Alaska, the Yukon, the Canadian Barrens—were a popular adjunct of the Western throughout the pulp era. They appeared in nearly all of the Western pulps (they were especially prevalent in Western Story, *where "Enough Gold" first appeared), as well as in* Argosy, Adventure, Short Stories, *and other general-fiction magazines; and such publications as* North-West Romances *and* Complete Northwest Novel *were devoted entirely to stories of the frozen North. James B. Hendryx, William Byron Mowery, and Robert Ormond Case, among others, built substantial careers specializing in this type of yarn. Such important Western writers as William MacLeod Raine, Luke Short, and Dan Cushman also wrote Northerns.*

W. Ryerson Johnson, a former coal miner and prolific contributor of both Westerns and Northerns to all the major pulp titles in the thirties and forties, was as adept as anyone at capturing the lusty flavor of life on the Far North frontier. His special area of expertise was the Canadian Barrens, an area in which he spent some time during a widely traveled youth. Johnson's pulp career lasted more than twenty years—and his literary career is now well into its sixth decade. In addition to his pulp output, he has published an impressive variety of stories and articles in such diverse magazines as This Week, Reader's Digest, Coronet *(a Northern short story, one of their rare uses of fiction),* Parent's Magazine, *and* Ellery Queen's Mystery Magazine. *Among his novels are two Westerns,* South to Sonora *(1946) and* Barb Wire *(1947), both of which were originally published as pulp serials.*

For seven long days and nights the wind had poured out of the Great Canadian Barrens, bending the tall spruces under its blast and piling snow high over the Dolomite Hills. And now the storm had blown itself out. White silence gripped the North.

Halfway up the slope, in a shake cabin several hundred feet above No-name Creek, ore so rich that it revealed more gold than quartz lay shimmering in a high yellow heap on the split-log table.

Big Ed Dekker sat and watched it. He looked bored and unhappy. Once in a while he reached out toward the golden pile and scooped up a handful. Sullenly he would hold it in his hand long enough to get the feel of its solid weight, then drop it back on the tabletop.

But most of the time he sat morosely and stared.

On the other hand his partner, I-like-fish Farrington, looked contented. Or at the very least, philosophically resigned. All it took to please him, apparently, was an empty tin can. He held the can in his hands and turned it around and around. The tough skin of his fingers made a monotonous *shuf-shuffing* sound against the paper wrapper. His lips moved soundlessly.

Suddenly those moving lips formed words out loud.

"Often it serve," he muttered. "Often it serve."

Ed Dekker looked up, startled, from his contemplation of the gold. Seeing his partner's hard-staring eyes, and the lips again making soundless movement, he began to feel goose flesh prickling out on him.

"You gone nuts?" he barked.

I-like-fish, usually shortened to Finny by Ed, who had invented the name in the first place, answered in a dead flat tone. No expression at all to the words, and less sense.

He said: "Often it serve delicious and wholesome packed freshly and waters Alaskan cold in caught is salmon brand iceberg."

"Crazy as a loon!" Ed Dekker blared. "Cooped up here all winter, with nothin' to see but white, nothin' to hear but silence, nothin' to eat but salmon out of cans! It's got you shakin' hands with the willows."

"Often it serve," Finny repeated solemnly.

Ed pushed to his feet so fast his stool thumped over backward. "It ain't enough I got to eat canned fish three times a day all winter when I don't like it anyway, but I got to listen to you read the labels all the time tellin' how good it is! And now you can't even read the label straight! I stood enough of your jabber. I stood too much." He came at his partner in a bull rush, long arms flailing.

Finny went down under that unexpected attack. But he didn't stay down. He popped up like a cork in water, swiped the back of his hand across his bloodied nose, and bored in with both fists.

Ed Dekker was a six-footer with a pair of shoulders on him that would have done credit to a mountain grizzly. But I-like-fish Farrington was big, too, and what slight disadvantage he lost in weight he made up in speed.

Toe to toe, they stood and rocked each other with their blows. Hard, bare-knuckled *thups* to the face and chest, and both of them standing into it, not giving an inch.

They had to fight. All the tension pent up through a long winter of getting on each other's nerves seemed to be released in this close-in hammering.

They didn't feel anything at all. The white months, gnawing their sanity to a thin shrill edge, seemed to have made them impervious to hurt. They might have gone on, absorbing fist jolts until one of them dropped from exhaustion, except that the tipped-over stool got in the way. Ed tripped over it and careened, pulling Finny with him. They hauled up against the table with its high heap of golden ore.

Ed, Finny, the table, and the gold crashed to the floor in a confused jumble.

Sitting in the wreckage of their own making, the partners blinked at each other with dawning comprehension of their folly. They were lifelong friends and here they were fighting. Over nothing.

With a guilty pang Ed recalled the cause of his suddenly aroused fury—Finny's aimless babbling. The white and silent North had caught up with Finny. For a long while it had been a toss-up which of them would crack first. Now Finny had cracked.

A feeling of overwhelming responsibility fell to Ed. Finny would have to be humored, babied even, until a period of association with fellow creatures in less hostile country had set his mind on sane tracks again. And instead of humoring the poor fellow he had started a fight with him!

He sought earnestly to make amends. "Finny, old-timer, I was only funnin' with you."

Finny nodded. "Yeah, I know."

"Salmon's good food," Ed declared. "I like it."

Finny nodded again, "Oven moderate in minutes twenty baked when delicious."

Ed reached out and patted him on the shoulder. "Now you jus' take it easy, Finny old boy."

"You understand what I said?" Finny demanded.

"Sure," Ed said pityingly.

"What did I say?"

Ed scratched at his stubbled jaw. "You said—"

"No use," Finny taunted. "You're too near bushed from sittin' lookin' at the gold every day. You'd never understand me."

"I could try," Ed said tolerantly.

"I was recitin' what the label on the salmon can said."

"That's—what the salmon can said, huh?"

"Sure. Backward."

"Huh?"

"I was memorizin' it backward."

A wild light mounted in Ed's eyes. "You mean you said them words like that on purpose?"

"Nothin' else. Cooped up here all winter with you, that's how I keep from losin' my mind. And if you don't stop broodin' over the gold and get to concentratin' on somethin' like a salmon-can label, you're gonna end up bushed as a dingbat."

"Well, I'm a flat-horned moose!" Ed growled. "Here I thought *you* were bushed, and I'm feelin' sorry for you." His big hand, the same which had patted Finny so sympathetically, doubled into a fist.

Finny dodged the blow and grinned. "We better get our gold swept up," he said.

While they scraped and picked to clear the floor of its golden flood, they talked more amiably than they had in weeks.

"With New Year's long gone a chinook should be blowin' down on us any time now," Finny volunteered. "We wouldn't have to wait for spring. Warm wind out of Oregon would melt enough of this snow in a day so we could maybe take our map and check off enough landmarks to locate the treasure."

"Yeah, if there is any treasure."

"What you mean by that? You were the one that wanted to stay in here this winter. I said we got enough gold, let's get out. You said there's no such thing as enough gold."

"I know. But the more I sit here all winter eatin' salmon and listenin' to you read the labels, the more I think we're a couple dopes to put so much trust in an Indian we never seen till jus' before he died."

"That Chippewyan didn't have any reason to fool us," Finny argued. "We come on him when he was dyin'. We chased off the man that shot him. Then we stayed with him and nursed him right to the end. Indians like to pay back. Only thing he had to give us was the map. I never doubted the map. All I doubted was the wisdom of us casin' up in these wolf-howlin' hills all through a starvation winter when we already had enough gold to make it easy for us on south."

They were filling the last of the pokes with the gold ore when suddenly, amazingly, the door rattled to a hard pounding outside.

"Hallo in there," a muffled voice called.

The two men swapped startled glances.

"Are we both off our nuts?" Finny whispered.

"Nope," Ed said, "we really heard it. I don't quite believe it, that's all. Lookin' at your loose-hung mug all winter, and I was forgettin' there's human bein's left in the world."

"Who'n hell could it be?" wondered Finny.

"We might try openin' the door and findin' out," Ed observed. "Could be a *mèti* I guess, wanderin' in to tail him out a new fur path."

The door rattled to a renewed banging.

Ed started moving toward the door. "If he's another label reader I'll jump on his face and make him swallow a can of salmon whole and unopened!" Looking back, he whispered hoarsely, "Stow that gold quick, Finny. With no guns, I wouldn't trust even a missionary."

"You're so danged suspicious," Finny grumbled, "sometimes I wonder if you even trust me."

He kicked the caribou-hide pokes under the bunk and Ed opened the door.

The man who tumbled inside, spattering snow in all directions, was a little man. His only observable feature in that first moment were his eyes. They were peculiar. They blazed from the depths of his fur dicky hood with a fixed, unblinking expression like an animal's.

His voice fit those oddly insensitive eyes. It was flat, impersonal, carrying an animallike purr.

"You fellas are a lifesaver to me," he said, his mouth cracking into a smile that didn't supply any warmth, but seemed mechanical almost to the point of inhumanness.

While the stranger peeled out of his bearskin mitts and parka, the partners stared at him in sober speculation.

"I'm Hymie Fess," the little man volunteered. "Rovin' free trader."

Out from under the parka and a Hudson's Bay mackinaw he moved toward the sheet-iron stove with the quick-muscled ease of a squirrel.

"Been lookin' over these creeks," he went on. "Had an idea I might spot some trappers in here an grubstake 'em." His thin lips twisted, showing glimpses of tiny pointed teeth. "Ain't enough fur in here to line a vest pocket! Devil's own country, these Dolomites. I lost my pack and rifle in a storm, and I ain't et for two days. If I hadn't run onto you boys—" He sliced his hand in a suggestive movement across his neck and made a disagreeable clucking noise.

"We lost our own guns when we first come in here late fall," Finny said sympathetically, "If we hadn't landed on this cabin, your bones wouldn't be the only ones stickin' outta the snow next May."

"You mean you got no guns at all?"

It was a natural enough question under the circumstances, but Ed, who had been trying to down an impression of menace ever since Hymie Fess had tumbled inside the door, quit trying to reason it aside, and flashed Finny a quick, warning glance.

But Finny reasoned that if the stranger was going to stay with them any length of time, he'd find out about the guns anyway. And in the meantime Hymie Fess was a welcome break in the monotony of their living. So he ignored Ed's warning.

"No guns," he said. "Don't matter much. Like you said, nothing back in here this season to shoot anyway."

"What have you been livin' on then?" Fess asked.

Ed answered that one. Scowling. "Canned salmon—entire and complete."

Finny pointed to the dark side of the cabin. "Take a look."

Hymie Fess left the stove and moved close. His eyes bulged out like peeled grapes when he saw can after can of salmon stacked against the wall.

"Hell! You been livin' like kings."

"Eat nothin' but salmon every day for as long as we have," Ed said sourly, "and you won't call it livin' like kings. You won't even call it livin'."

"I like fish," Finny explained. "But Ed here would take the whole shebang for three beans or a prune."

Hymie Fess couldn't seem to take his eyes away from the salmon. He ran his tongue over his slack lips hungrily. Finny opened a can for him and Fess started wolfing the salmon, sounding a note of animal contentment from somewhere deep in his throat.

"Dry, ain't it?" he said finally, swallowing hard.

"It's some special dry pack, I guess," Finny told him. "So the can'll stand plenty of cold without bustin'."

"How come you to lug 'em all in here?" the little man asked curiously.

"We didn't," Ed horned in. "We inherited 'em."

"There was a gold-prospectin' party in here last year," Finny explained. "They put up this cabin, such as it is. Someone must have made the feller in charge a deal on a carload of salmon. Anyhow the fish was brought in here to feed a whole crew of men. But the crew never was imported because the vein pinched out. When the prospectin' party went south, salmon bein' too heavy to carry, they left most of it here."

"We heard about it from an Indian," Ed threw in.

"With no gold and no fur in here," Hymie Fess questioned, with his mouth full of salmon, "why the hell did you fellas stay all winter?"

Ed made up a plausible lie. "We got a prospect on farther north," he said. "We want to be all set to jump soon's the snow's off the ground."

"Speakin' of snow off the ground," Hymie Fess grunted,

"won't be long, I'm thinkin'. Chinook blowin' down on us. I can feel it in my bones."

Ed and Finny both nodded agreement to that, and Hymie Fess looked up from the table, swiping the back of his hand two ways across his mouth. "Eat some more," Finny urged.

"Enough for now." The little man's predatory glance probed the corners of the cabin. The fingers of one hand drummed on the table top. It was the other hand which caught Ed's eye. He pretended not to see when Hymie Fess thrust his long fingernails in a crack of the table top and pinched out a few tiny flakes of gold.

Ed went over and took his mackinaw down from a peg. "Think I'll step outside for some fresh air. Salmon smell's gettin' too thick for me."

For the next two days the intense cold held, with the wind blowing in blustery gusts from out of the north. Hymie Fess had made himself at home in the cabin. Although there was nothing that could rightly be called suspicious about his actions, even Finny came to feel uneasy in his presence.

The little man, with his oddly fixed eyes, seemed to ooze an attitude of waiting. He seemed strangely like a cat at a game trail. Ed and Finny contrived never to leave him alone in the cabin.

On the morning of the third day they awoke, all three of them, sweltering under their blankets.

"Chinook!" Ed cried.

He bolted out of his bunk and threw the door open wide. Under the drive of a bland southwest wind the snow was melting before his very eyes. From the eaves of the cabin water fell in a steady drip. Inside the cabin, too. The whole floor was puddled from the leaking roof.

"What is this, a cabin or a sieve?" Hymie Fess grumbled.

"Somebody slapped it together pretty fast all right," Finny agreed. "Two-three times this winter we thought the wind would toss us down the gulch in back."

All that day and the next and the next the wind blew warm and strong. The sun shone, too, and between the unseasonable wind and the sun, the snow continued to vanish as though by magic. Patches of bare black rock appeared on the slope below the cabin. Above it a nest of dolomite boulders poked through. Big Fellows. Big as a cabin, some of them.

Both Ed and Finny had memorized the map which pointed the way to the burial place of Chippewyan treasure. They did the best they could to conceal from Hymie Fess their avid interest in the melting away of the snow blanket which all winter had concealed the landmarks indicated on the map.

By now some of these landmarks were unmistakably revealed. The partners conferred nervously with each other whenever they could get a few minutes out from under the patiently watchful eyes of Hymie Fess. They trusted Hymie less than ever now. On the first morning of the chinook he had produced a revolver from a concealed shoulder holster and had spent the greater part of the day polishing it and testing its action.

"Thought you'd lost your guns," Ed threw at him.

"All but this one." Hymie's voice was an animallike purr.

All in all, Hymie Fess was fast becoming the partner's number-one problem. How they were going to go about tracking down the treasure with the sly little man eternally watching them was worrying Ed and Finny more than they wanted to admit.

Hymie didn't help their ease of mind by something he said one day. Gazing out at the new contours uncovered in the rugged Dolomite Hills by the melting snow, he remarked unemotionally, "If anyone had a map and they were waitin' for the snow to go, so's to check off landmarks, now'd be the time, wouldn't it?"

Just before dark on the third day of the warm winds something happened to divert the partners' minds from their growing worry. Water was trickling in tiny rivulets everywhere and suddenly, from a little way up the steep slope, a bank of snow let go. It *swooshed* past the cabin in a sinuous flow, a miniature avalanche, down, on down four hundred feet until it disappeared over a precipice into the gorge below.

In passing, it loosened the cribbed slide rock which had been thrown up as a foundation for the cabin. The cabin developed a pronounced sag, and Ed, Finny, and Hymie Fess, all three, worked like beavers until long after dark bolstering the shaky structure.

Then they each ate a can of salmon—Hymie Fess with evident relish, Finny with resignation, Ed with blasphemous mutterings and facial contortions registering acute displeasure—and piled into their blankets.

The last thing Ed said before he went to sleep was, "I can't choke down another bite—never. I wisht an avalanche would cart away every last can of salmon we got in the place."

None of them slept well that night. The temperature stayed above freezing and hour after black hour water everywhere dripped and gurgled. Several times the slurring roar of a snowslide echoed from nearby hills.

The gray smudge of dawn was in the sky when Ed and Hymie Fess were awakened, and Finny was thrown clear of his bunk by a crashing jolt which shook the whole cabin.

"Some of them dolomite boulders up above has let go!" Finny diagnosed the case.

The three men crowded for the door in the bare nick of time. Another splintering crash slewed the cabin three feet around on its slide rock base, and precipitated the partners and Hymie Fess out the door on their faces.

They scrambled to their feet with the sound of that splintering still loud in their ears. Down the slope, echoing away from them, they could hear the pounding thud of the unseated boulder which had slewed the cabin around as it made its way to the oblivion of the gorge below.

No more rocks came tumbling, and Finny stuck his head

inside the door. He looked out again quickly. There was enough light in the morning sky to show his face, gray and shaken.

"You've got your wish, Ed," was all he said.

"Huh? How you mean?"

"Take a look for yourself. That last chunk of rock knocked the whole side of the cabin out. Every last can of salmon is avalanched clear to the bottom of the gorge. The gold, too, that was under the bunk."

Working frantically, they cleared the cabin of their remaining gear, then waited miserably for the sun to poke its first red fingers between the high hills. In the full light of the day Ed examined the gaping hole in the side of the tilted cabin and did some emergency shoring while Finny scoured the slope for some sign of a salmon can or a glint of the golden ore.

Finny didn't find anything. The sliding snow and rock had swept clean, carrying everything down and dumping it into the inaccessible gorge below. He dragged wearily back to the cabin and Ed read the answer in his dull eyes.

Neither of them said anything, but both realized they were so close to death that it was all over but the dying. The chinook would blow itself out and winter would clamp down again. It would be six weeks at least before they could get out of these starvation Dolomite Hills. Six weeks. And all they had to eat was a handful of tea leaves which Ed had garnered leaf by leaf from the cabin wreckage. They'd be lucky to last six days.

"Anyhow it'll be a relief not to have to eat no more salmon," Ed said, with a faint grin.

In the tragic awareness of their greater loss neither of them gave any thought to the gold. Nor to Hymie Fess. All morning the hardeyed little man had sat on a rock and watched silently, offering no help.

Now suddenly his rasping voice jerked Ed and Finny to realization of other things besides the loss of their food.

"Look around, you two dimwits!"

The same thought leaped to both of them. On the slope above, from where the dolomite boulder had rolled down to wreck the cabin, there was another huge boulder perilously balanced. Hymie Fess, they thought, must be sounding a warning about it.

They looked around, and there was the boulder the same as ever. And there was Hymie Fess with no more expression on his face than it had ever showed. But he was covering them with his revolver.

"I want the map," he said tersely.

"What map?" asked Finny.

"The only map there is. The one you got off the Chippewyan."

"What're you talkin' about?" Finny asked dully.

"Don't stall," Hymie Fess snarled. "It was dark. You didn't see me so good, I guess. But I saw you. I snuck back after you'd took my guns and chased me off. I watched you in the light of your campfire. I wasn't outfitted to hang close on your trail. It took me a while. But I found you." The revolver moved threateningly. "Hand over that map!"

"So you were the one!" Ed slashed. "I thought there was somethin' about you—you were the one who was torturin' the Chip—"

Hymie Fess growled like an animal ready to spring. "The map!"

"Here it is." Finny reached inside his clothes, pulled out a folded piece of thin caribou hide. He tossed it, and Hymie Fess caught and unfolded the native-cured parchment with one hand.

Out of the tail of his eyes he examined it and grunted in quick satisfaction.

"I'll let you live till I check on this," he told the two partners. "Hadn't ought to take long. Looks like the Indian's buried his treasure close."

"Won't do you no more good'n it's doin' us," Finny said, in apathetic warning.

"Oh, yeah? Why won't it?"

"Because there's nothin' to eat. You'll never get out of the Dolomites without food."

"Looks like I'm way ahead of you on that," Hymie Fess said softly.

Finny frowned. "How d'you mean?"

The little man chuckled malevolently. "If it comes to that, there's always you two."

Ed was nodding quietly. He knew it about this little man from the first, he was telling himself. Hymie Fess was the kind eminently fitted to survive in this country. No more feelings, no more sensitivity than a hungry animal.

Hymie Fess put it into words. "I been noticin' you close. I estimate you two would dress down to a couple hundred pounds, easy, of nourishin' meat."

They watched him as he backed away with the revolver. At a little distance he turned and strode along, cocky as a wolverine that has buried a fat carcass in anticipation of another day's hunger. They watched him stoop to grab up one of their own miner's picks, then disappear around a snow-pillowed shoulder of gray granite.

Alone, they stared at each other.

"We could follow him," Finny suggested doubtfully.

"Maybe it'd be better to wait for him here," Ed rumbled.

"He might not come back," Finny said thoughtfully. "If it's like he said, that he's been on our trail instead of just stumbling in here accidentally while lookin' over the creeks for fur, then he's probably got a cache of food somewhere near. I remember thinkin' that first day he showed in that he didn't eat much salmon for a starvin' man."

"I caught that, too," Ed told him. "That's why I went outside to look at his tracks before the wind buried 'em. I found his pack and I took it and hid it."

Finny's voice kindled with new interest. "And you never said nothin' about it to me?"

"You know how it's been between us, cooped up here all winter. We ain't either one been givin' the other credit for a lick of horse sense. With Hymie Fess not showin' actually hostile, I was afraid you'd think I was bushed as a loon for being so suspicious of him. You been crabbin' all your life I'm too suspicious. So I thought I'd wait a little while and see how he turned out. But he was waitin', too. And now it's too late for anything, looks like."

"Maybe not," Finny said with growing excitement. "There's a pack, you said. With food—"

"There was a pack," Ed corrected dismally. "When the chinook came, the pack got washed out from where I hid it. It's playin' tag now down in the gulch with our salmon."

"All right," said Finny, accepting the inevitable, "it's gone. We'll have to think of somethin' else. But when Hymie Fess misses it he'll come back here—"

"To kill us and eat us!"

"Yeah." Finny rubbed his gloved hand against his stubbled jaw. There was a speculative look in his eyes.

"You thinkin' about the same thing I am?" growled Ed.

"Guess so," Finny said slowly. "I'm wonderin' how hungry we'd have to get before it would be a pleasure to bite into Hymie Fess."

"It'd be about as appetizin' a meal as some barbwire dipped in rattlesnake poison," Ed declared. "I'd sooner even eat salmon."

"Well, whether we eat him or not," Finny said practically, "we can't just squat here and leave him eat us."

Ed's bleak glance was ranging upward in the direction of the dolomite boulders uncovered by the melting snow. When the big one which had wrecked the cabin had let go, it had sheered a slice of the gravel slope off with it, creating a stable level except for the solitary boulder which half overhung the scalped slope near the top.

Finny was noticing where Ed's glance held. His eyes glinted. "I think we got somethin' there," he breathed.

Ed swore softly in that breathless way a man does when he's got the answer to something so pat that he won't quite let himself believe it.

"Maybe I'm a shade quicker'n you," Finny observed. "I better work down here and you take the top."

"All the danger's down here," Ed grumbled. "I might start an avalanche that would bury you both."

"I think most of the loose stuff's already gone down. The boulder is all. I'll be watchin' close. I can duck it."

"What if he ducks it, too? He's quick as lightnin'."

"Leave him duck. All I'll be lookin' for is to shift his attention long enough to grab his gun."

"You be careful," Ed warned, gruff concern in his voice.

"Sure."

"I mean careful."

"Sure."

When Hymie Fess-came back, Finny was bent over pretending to be doing something with rocks. If Hymie Fess wanted to have good footing when he braced Finny with the revolver there was only one place for him to stand. Everywhere else around, the partners had piled snow or pried rocks on edge.

So Fess stood where they wanted him to, with his back to the slope and on a dead line with the boulder. Finny heard him, of course, but he pretended not to. He didn't look up until Hymie Fess started to curse him.

Then Finny straightened as though in surprise. "Why, what's the matter, Hymie? Seems like a man that had just annexed a treasure would be a mite happy and pleased about it."

Hymie was standing a few feet away, his revolver leveled and all, his wiry body—with the exception, strangely enough, of the hand which held the gun—quivering in rage. His face grimaced, the thin lips working over the pointed teeth.

Finny looked at him in amazement that was not at all feigned. "Didn't you find the treasure, Hymie?"

"I found it," the little man snarled.

"Wasn't there enough gold to suit you? Or what?"

"There wasn't any gold! And if you don't do some tall talkin' before I count to three, I'll feed a slug through your wide mouth just as a warnin' to your partner that Hymie Fess don't stand for monkeyshines. I'm countin'. One . . . two—"

Finny took his cap off and scratched at his head. Ed, watching anxiously for this signal, popped into view from his rocky covert above and gave the boulder a push.

"Look out behind you!" Finny bellowed as Hymie Fess's mouth was pursed to say "three."

Hymie Fess could plainly hear the crashing slam of the boulder as it bounced downward, so he knew Finny's warning wasn't faked.

He blazed a single shot, but his body was jerking when he pulled the trigger, and so was Finny's. So the first shot did no good—or no harm, according to the point of view.

The boulder which Ed had unloosened was as big as a table, and the clattering crash it made sounded louder by the split second. There was no getting away from it; Hymie Fess had to risk a look upward to see which way to jump. That was where Finny had it on him. Finny had been in position to see how the boulder was rolling from the start. He knew before Fess knew it, which way the little man would jump.

Consequently he was there a wink ahead of Hymie.

The breath was half knocked out of the venomous little man as he collided with Finny. He must have thought the boulder had caught up with him after all, because he screamed like any stricken animal. At the same time he blazed another shot from his gun.

The bullet and the boulder slammed past in the same breath, and Hymie Fess tipped over backward with Finny riding him down. Finny's solid weight was too much for Hymie, and this time the other half of his breath was knocked out of him. Finny landed a right and a left to the jaw to make sure Hymie stayed out for a while. Then, prying the revolver from Hymie's nerveless fingers, he stood up, roaring in triumph to Ed, who was clumping down the slope, leaving a young avalanche in the wake of his seven-league strides.

"Nice goin'," Ed shouted, puffing. "Nice goin', Finny."

Finny shook his head, sobering down. "Somethin's way wrong. Hymie Fess found where the treasure was supposed to be. That Chippewyan must have been havin' a pipe dream. No gold there, Hymie claimed."

Ed stared lugubriously. "Hell, and after us stayin' up here all winter eatin' canned salmon—Hey, wait a minute!" Sudden joy lighted his face. "Somethin' I forgot to tell you. Look."

A few long strides carried him to their tin-can dump just outside the cabin. His gloved hands dived into the pile, and after a few minutes' searching he brought up a can from underneath, brushed off the snow, hurried back to Finny, and put the can in his hands.

The can plummeted from Finny's hands before he could look at it. It simply bored through his loosened grasp, like a lead weight falling, and sank into the snow.

Finny picked it up and pulled open the loose jagged lid. The bright sun played on the contents, bringing out soft yellow glints.

"Gold ore!" Finny gasped.

Ed was watching him, grinning. "Sure."

"Where in blazes did it come from?"

"It's ours. The same we been hoardin' all winter. Hidin' Hymie Fess's pack wasn't the only thing I done. I took our gold from under the bunk and put it in the tin cans for safe keepin'. I figured if it came to a showdown, old tin cans out in plain sight would be the last place Fess would think to look for gold."

"Then . . . then last night when the rock hit, our gold never went down the gulch with the salmon!"

"Nope. It's every bit in these cans."

"Looks like you mighta told a fella somethin' about it," Finny said a little resentfully.

Ed shrugged. "What was the use? With our food gone, it didn't seem very important." The animation drained out of his face. "Hell, it ain't important now, is it? For a minute I was forgettin'."

"Me, too," said Finny glumly.

"Gold or no gold, without food we're—"

"Goners," Finny completed the thought for him.

The wind was beginning to change, they both noticed. It was a cold wind, a foretaste of the gale that soon would be hurling fresh snow out of the north to smother all trace of the chinook's bland warmth.

Hymie Fess had been moaning. Now he sat up unsteadily.

Ed looked balefully at the little man. "I don't think I could ever do it," he told Finny, shaking his head hopelessly. "I believe I'd sooner eat more salmon."

"Salmon," Hymie Fess moaned. "Salmon—might be treasure to a Chippewyan—but it's only canned fish to me."

The partners both jumped at him. They slapped and shook him back to full consciousness. "What's that you're sayin'?" Ed demanded.

"I thought it was gold," Hymie Fess blubbered. "The Chip admitted he swiped a treasure fom the prospectin' party in here and cached it in a cave. I made him draw me a map. Naturally I thought he meant gold. I just now found the cave. *And it's full of salmon. Nothin' but salmon!*"

A look of philosophical calm passed over I-like-fish Farrington's face.

Ed Dekker seemed stunned. "Salmon the on bring," he croaked weakly. "Often it serve—often it serve!"

I.O.U.—ONE BULLET

Dan Cushman

SOME *pulp writers specialized in one type of story, set in the same general locale. Other pulpsters, like Max Brand and Dan Cushman, preferred to write stories of different types, utilizing a wide variety of global settings. Cushman's substantial pulp output in the forties and early fifties consisted of Western, adventure, and historical tales, with occasional forays into other categories, and his settings included the jungles of Africa, the frozen wastes of the Far North, the byways of the mysterious Orient, the timber country of the northern U.S. and southern Canada, and the frontier of his adopted state of Montana.*

"I.O.U.—One Bullet," which first appeared in Lariat Story Magazine *in 1946, is a good example of Cushman's Western pulp fiction—lean, well-characterized, suspenseful, and unconventional in both subject matter and handling. Those same characteristics distinguish his novels, the most famous of which is* Stay Away, Joe, *a hilarious and yet honest and moving portrait of a group of American Indians which was a major book-club selection and a bestseller in 1953. Another of his fine humorous novels is* The Old Copper Collar *(1957), a tumultous tale of politics and similar shenanigans in nineteenth-century Montana. Outstanding among his more traditional Westerns are* Montana, Here I Be! *(1950),* North Fork to Hell *(1964), and the recent* Rusty Irons *(Walker, 1984). He has also published a number of adventure novels, a nonfiction history of* The Great North Trail, *and a play—* Whoop-Up—*adapted from* Stay Away, Joe *and produced in 1958.*

Kellan was sheriff at Jug Springs. He was a good sheriff—after his own fashion. No prisoner was ever known to have escaped him, once Kellan got within range. Dead men don't run, and that was the way Kellan liked to bring in his prisoners. Dead, with a little round bullet hole right between the eyes. Kellan felt that he had performed his duties with praiseworthy thoroughness when that bullet hole was placed in the geometrical center of a prisoner's forehead.

"Shot trying to escape!" Kellan would announce, and that would be the end of it. Nobody argued much with Kellan.

The second time Kellan ran for sheriff he was defeated. The winner was Dad Banks—willing enough, and nervy enough, though nothing like the superb marksman that Kellan was. Kellan surprised everyone by accepting his defeat with a shrug and one of his rare smiles. He made it a point to shake hands with Dad Banks in public, and ask for the job of undersheriff. Once it was learned Kellan wanted to be undersheriff, there were no other applicants. He got the job. A month or so later, Dad Banks was found shot to death in the alley behind the Virginia Saloon. The bullet had made its mark right in the middle of Dad's forehead. After that Kellan took to wearing the sheriff's badge again, and next election he ran unopposed.

He was a tall man, Kellan, rangy but not big muscled. He carried a finely made .41 calibre revolver in the middle of his waist with the butt pointed to the right side, and in his right-hand coat pocket he always had one of those old-time cap-and-ball .44 derringers. It would have been uselesss for Kellan to carry a gun for his left hand—he couldn't have shot it, because the thumb and forefinger of that left hand had been amputated long before. However, in Kellan's case, the right hand was sufficient.

It was March during the first year of Kellan's third term. The season's customary raw wind cut down the long, wandering main street of Jug Springs, and rattled the new sign above the side entrance of the Central Montana Territorial Bank.

Edward J. Horn
ATTORNEY AT LAW

A young man was standing beneath the piece of flapping metal, looking at it from critical angles. Finally he seemed to be satisfied. It was a good sign, gold letters against black, and it had been hung evenly. Edward J. Horn, Attorney at Law! The young man squared his rather narrow shoulders, cleared his throat after the manner of a judge on the bench, and laughed.

"You think it's funny too, son?"

The speaker was gray-whiskered Dixie Skelton, retired prospector and prominent Jug Springs whiskey bum.

The young man rubbed his chin for a thoughtful moment. "No," he decided. "I don't think it's exactly funny."

"I think it's funny," said Dixie. "When I seen it there about an hour ago, I busted right out." And to prove this, Dixie whacked his thigh with the palm of his hand, beating dirt from his sourdough pants. "He! He! I sure do think it's funny."

"What's so funny about that sign?"

"Why, the idee of a lawyer settin' up business here in Jug Springs. We never get a case as far as to the courts in this camp. That is, nothin' except fist fighters, and now and then a small thief."

"No enforcement?"

This brought a snort from Dixie. "No enforcement? Reckon we got a whole heap of enforcement. Kellan shoots 'em all as soon as he gets in range. Says he shoots 'em tryin' to escape."

"And who, may I ask, is Kellan?" asked the lawyer.

The droop of Dixie's gray-stubbled chin indicated his

amazement. Dixie had run across men who had never heard of George Washington, or President Grant, maybe, but none who had not heard of Kellan. Not lately, anyhow.

"Kellan," he said, "is lord high sheriff here in Jug Springs. Been so for about five year now. Say, who are you that you ain't heard tell of Kellan? You must come from 'way back East in Minnesoty, or Ioway, or someplace."

"I," said the young man, gesturing at the sign, "am Edward J. Horn, and I come from Pennsylvania."

"So you're the lawyer. Son, take my advice and move on to greener range. Jug Springs ain't no place for you. Take Helena, now—that's the capital of this territory. That's a town where lawyers get fat as prairie dogs in a cornfield. Stick here, and you'll likely have to take up sheepherdin' for a sideline before the summer's over."

Ed Horn laughed. Jug Springs, Helena—what was the difference? One place was as good as another as far as he was concerned. He'd had an unfortunate love affair back in Pennsylvania a little while before, and consequently the world seemed weary and futile. Besides, he didn't give much credence to what Dixie was telling him. Nobody could conduct an office like Dixie said Kellan did. So Ed Horn only laughed.

In the weeks to come, he learned that a great deal of what Dixie said about Kellan was true. However, it didn't worry him much until that day that Riggs Purdy came to town.

Riggs was a suspected cattle rustler, a confirmed loafer, and no credit to the community. He had a little two-bit spread out by the Turtle Hills, a corral, a shanty, a wife, and three or four rag-tail kids. Kellan had once warned Riggs to stay away from the Jug Springs country, but that had been four years before, and four years is a long time.

Riggs was just coming from the door of Annie's Saloon when Kellan started across the street. They saw each other about the same time. A fraction of a second later the .41 barked in Kellan's hand. Riggs hadn't even gone for his gun.

He just rolled over his toes and went down across the plank sidewalk. Kellan strode over, long-legged, his loose coat flapping in the wind. The wind always seemed to blow in Jug Springs. He turned Riggs part way over with the toe of his boot, and smiled a little when he saw that the bullet had centered right between the eyes.

That night there was a meeting at Ed Horn's office. The men who attended came singly, their hats pulled over their eyes, and mostly they came by way of the back stairs. The light burned until late, then, at one of the hours between midnight and dawn, a dozen masked men strode through the lobby of the Western hotel, climbed to the second floor, and knocked at the door to Kellan's room.

When the sheriff came to the door, Ed spoke briefly. "Kellan, this is the Jug Springs Vigilance Committee. We had a meeting tonight and voted unanimously that the office of sheriff is now vacant. The field is open for candidates, but we'd advise you not to be one of them."

That was all. Kellan did not argue. There was only one type of argument that Kellan understood, and the collection of sawed-off shotguns and Colt pistols which were pointed in his direction ruled that argument out of order. Next morning his badge was found lying on the desk of the sheriff's office—but he still carried the .41 revolver, and the .44 derringer in his coat pocket on the right side.

Kellan spent the days that followed brooding over a bottle in the Western bar. He had nothing to say about the vigilance committee, but several persons noticed that his eyes would become as hard as gray quartz whenever Horn came in sight, and sometimes the long muscles of his gun arm would tighten, and his fingers would twitch.

One evening Horn strolled up to the bar at the Westen to have a drink with friends. After a moment they seemed to forget about Kellan who was sitting at his favorite table at the rear. In the course of the conversation which followed, one of the men at the bar said something about cowards. Horn had a theory on cowards, too—purely philosophical, nothing to give offense to anyone, but Kellan, overhearing him, arose slowly and strode over to tap him on the elbow. Kellan tapped him, not with his gun hand, but with the one which had the thumb and forefinger missing.

"I overheard you say something about what makes a man a coward. It just happens that I have an opinion on that, too. When I was young, I lived up in the lumber woods of Michigan. In that country a man was supposed to fight with his fists. A man was called a coward if he packed a gun. But out here in the territories we have a different code. We call a man a coward if he *doesn't* carry a gun. And here's something more, Mister Lawyer, we call men cowards who go in gangs and hide behind masks. In other words, Horn, in my opinion that makes you a coward."

With a smile, Horn drew a derringer and laid it on the bar.

"This may not be much of a gun, Kellan, but you're wrong in thinking I go around unarmed. And right while we're on the subject of cowards, I don't mind saying that I think you're the worst coward in Jug Springs."

"In what way?"

"Because you kill men without giving them a chance. Oh, I know!—they all get their chance to draw. That's a joke!" Horn laughed like it really was a joke. "What chance does that give a man against you?—you with a hand as fast as a rattlesnake, and as accurate as any circus shot in the country. I've often wondered how you would face death with the odds even for and against you."

Kellan glanced around the room, now grown silent, and perhaps a tiny smile twisted his lips. He took the .41 from its holster and passed it across to the bartender. Then he took his own derringer from his pocket and placed it on the bar close to Horn's.

"I'll give you a chance to find **out**," Kellan said. "I'll shoot it out with you—with derringers, at fifteen paces. Nobody can be sure where a derringer ball will go at that distance, so we'll have that even break you were talking about. We'll draw lots for the first shot. How does that sound to you, my brave young lawyer?"

"Kellan, I'm beginning to admire you. I didn't think you had a proposition like that in your system." He called to Harry the swamper, "Harry! Break a couple of straws off that broom and bring them here." The swamper obeyed. "Short one gets last shot, that all right by you, Kellan?"

"Yes."

They drew straws. Kellan's was the short one. Without a word he stepped off fifteen long paces. This carried him almost to the rear of the room. He stood, perfectly still, waiting. Horn steadied himself, took aim with his derringer, and pulled the trigger. The gun spat weakly, and its wandering bullet knocked plaster from the wall a foot to the right of Kellan's shoulder.

Kellan then inspected the load in his own derringer.

"Your turn," said Horn almost cheerfully.

The tone of the remark seemed to make Kellan wince. He paused for a while, looking up the room at the young lawyer. Finally, he slowly raised the derringer and took aim. Horn was still not perturbed. He smiled at Kellan and calmly munched a second pretzel. And, unexpectedly, Kellan lowered his gun.

"You don't seem afraid to die."

"Why, no. Now you mention it, I guess I'm not. However, I won't pretend that's because I'm especially brave. It's just— well, maybe because I haven't much to live for."

"Still, you'd like to live for a while."

"I wouldn't mind."

"I wouldn't mind, either. Should we let it lay this way— with you owing me a shot?"

"Any way you want it."

"All right, I have one shot coming. I'll be around to take it—sometime."

Kellan collected his .41 from the bartender and dropped

the derringer back in his right hand coat pocket. He was poker-faced, as usual, though now and then a little smile seemed to tickle the corners of his mouth—the kind of smile he used to wear after he had placed a bullet perfectly between his prisoner's eyes. He started for the door, but halfway outside he stopped having thought of something more he wanted to say to Ed Horn.

"Some day, lawyer, you may not be quite so happy to die as you were tonight."

For a week or two Jug Springs talked plenty about that bullet Ed Horn had coming from the barrel of Kellan's little .44 derringer, but Dixie Skelton, the whiskey bum, was the only one who came out and suggested to him a course that lots of people considered advisable.

"You ain't goin' to let that killer shoot at you whenever he wants?" Dixie asked.

"Whenever he wants," said Horn.

"He'd have to run down some steep canyons to pay back a bullet he owed me. Son, you take my advice and clear out of this camp. Light out at night and don't tell nobody where you're headed. That Kellan, he's pizen. He'll take that shot, and when he does you'll be a dead man."

But Ed only laughed. "Here's four-bits, Dixie. Buy yourself a couple of drinks. And don't worry about that shot of Kellan's—I guess nobody hits too close with a derringer at fifteen paces."

Months passed, and still Kellan did not collect. Jug Springs grew as a spur of the Montana Northern was built in. One morning Kellan checked out of the Western Hotel, tossing his grip into the boot of the southbound stage. He was going to Denver on a visit. Six months later he had not returned.

It was the following spring, April 15th to be exact, and the blossoms of Jug Springs's only apple tree, a stunted sugar crab, scented the air of the large, fenced-in front yard of Jeremy Albertson, storekeeper and influential citizen. Ed

Horn, portfolio in hand, was returning from a visit to the outlying shack of one of his clients, a sheepherder who had received broken bones and lacerations because of the neglect of other parties, and as a result was interested in receiving pecuniary solace through the courts. Horn, convinced of the right, had taken the sheepherder's case, had left a supply of advice and chewing tobacco, and had headed back to the office where he had an appointment with Matt Blake, banker. The blossoms of the sugar crab scented the thin air for a considerable distance, causing Horn to sniff and glance across the fence to Albertson's yard to discover the source.

What he saw there caused him to draw up quite suddenly, for, standing beside the gnarled, pink-tufted branches of the sugar crab, breaking blossom stems into an outspread apron, was the most beautiful girl he had ever seen. A vision in white dimity. A girl of such perfect proportions she could not be described as tall, short, thin, or otherwise—she was ideal.

Ed Horn set down his portfolio and manipulated the patent catch on the gate. A strange feeling, akin to paralysis, came over him when their eyes first met, and he walked most of the distance to the apple tree before words found their way from his lips.

"Is Mr. Albertson home?" he asked, knowing well enough old Jeremy would be absent from his store at the hour of eleven A.M., weekday, for no occasion less important than his own funeral.

"Father is at the store," answered the perfection in white.

Horn clucked his tongue regretfully. Afterward he smiled with the air of a man who is willing to accept such disappointment graciously.

"May I help you with your apple blossoms, Miss Albertson?" he asked.

"You know me! I'm sorry but I don't seem . . ." The girl cast down her eyes and seemed genuinely embarrassed that she had not recognized this man who was evidently an old acquaintance. "You see, I've been gone for a couple of years, and I've forgotten—"

"You haven't forgotten me," smiled Ed. "You never saw me before. You called Jeremy Albertson 'father,' and I was detective enough to see that must be your last name. Let's see now, I think I've heard him mention you. Your name is Alice—"

"Bernice."

"Bernice! Of course it would be Bernice. I think Bernice is the most beautiful name I've ever heard, and it fits you perfectly. But excuse me—I'm Ed Horn, struggling attorney . . ."

Ed Horn helped pick apple blossoms until the poor dwarf crab was almost denuded. He forgot his appointment with Matt Blake, banker. When Jeremy Albertson trudged home at noon, he was still there. He accepted an invitation to dinner—the noon meal in Jug Springs—and stayed on to assist in the spading of a pansy bed. He barely resisted an invitation to supper, but suggested that he return in the evening. This he did, with a hired top buggy, with tassels, coal oil reflector lamps, and extremely high wheels.

In the days that followed Horn moved with an air of one who has been elevated to a new and particularly delightful planet.

George Rathbone, freckled editor of the Jug Springs Trailblazer, weekly newspaper, saw how things were going and printed several subtle paragraphs in his column "Rambles with Ye Editor." But, about the first of June, Rathbone had something more definite to print, and the Trailblazer came from the hand press with front page bannering the "approaching Albertson-Horn nuptials."

The wedding was to take place on Sunday, June 16th at the Jug Springs community church. On the night of the 15th, Ed Horn and three of his friends turned in at the Western bar for a few drinks, "memorial to his bachelorhood."

A tenseness gripped the crowd at the Western when they saw who it was. The silence which settled seemed to have body to it; it seemed to be explosive; it was like a string drawn taut to the breaking point. Horn could feel that silence as he walked toward the bar.

Kellan! There sat Kellan at his favorite table near the back of the room. There was a bottle and an unconsumed glass of liquor in front of him. He made no move when Horn walked to the bar, there was no change in his expression, except, perhaps, for a little twist at the corners of his mouth. He was sitting away from the table a few inches so as to free the butt of his .41, and the right hand pocket of his floppy suit coat sagged, as always, beneath the weight of the .44 derringer.

After a quarter-minute or so, he spoke up, "Hello, Horn."

A few beads of quick perspiration had sprung to glisten along Horn's hairline. He looked at Kellan for a while before he could force himself to answer in a voice that had a cracked and hollow sound. "Hello, Kellan."

"You seem . . . surprised." Kellan talked slowly, separating his words with agonizing meticulousness. "Didn't you think I'd come back?"

Horn made a quick pass at the perspiration on his forehead. Kellan rose slowly on his long legs. "Or maybe you thought I had a poor memory. No, I have a good memory. Extremely good. And when I read that account of your wedding, I—"

One of Horn's companions broke in, "Kellan, for God's sake, you didn't come here after all this time expecting him to stand up against that wall while you shot at him."

Kellan went on as though he hadn't heard a word, "So when I read about your wedding, I thought to myself, 'Ed Horn is a brave man. He's an honest man, and he wouldn't want to get married with an important debt outstanding.' So, as soon as I saw the piece in the paper, I came, to settle up."

Horn's jaw was set, but he looked extremely pale in the light of the big hanging lamps.

"What's wrong, Horn?" Kellan smirked. "You don't seem

quite so indifferent as you did that other time. Aren't you as anxious to meet death the night before your wedding? Maybe you'd like to back down on your bargain?"

"I'm not backing down, Kellan!"

Still in no hurry, Kellan picked up the dish of pretzels on the bar and passed them. "As I recall, you enjoyed a pretzel or two that other night. Won't you have some?"

Horn ignored the pretzels. "Count off your fifteen paces," he said, starting to the rear of the room, but one of his companions seized him and swung him around.

"Don't be a fool, Ed. You don't have to stand back of that old bargain. Nobody will think any the less of you."

But Horn freed himself with a firm motion and continued on his way, stopping at about the same spot where Kellan had once stood. Kellan strode off his fifteen paces and slowly drew the .44 derringer from his coat pocket.

"Ready?" he asked.

"Yes."

He set himself, stood very straight, brought the barrel of the little gun level. He seemed in no hurry to fire. He wanted to make the moment last as long as possible. The tick-tick of the clock over the backbar was the only sound in the room. Kellan smiled a little, his finger grew tense over the trigger.

With a flame and roar like a buffalo gun, the derringer came to life in his hand.

Horn was untouched. A dozen pellets had rattled to the floor, and a couple had stung through his clothes, but there was no killing power in them.

Kellan, however, had dropped to his knees and was staring at his right hand, now shredded and bleeding. After a few seconds he climbed to his feet, staggered through the door, and across the street toward the doctor's office, leaving behind him a dribble of blood.

Five minutes later Dixie Skelton was rushing from bar to bar, collecting free drinks on the strength of a sensational piece of news.

"It was Kellan. He's down at the sawbone's now. Gun hand was blown off, except for the last couple of fingers. He loaded that old derringer up too heavy, that's what he did. Must have had an ounce of powder and an ounce of buck crammed into her. That's right—buckshot! He didn't aim on missin' the lawyer, Kellan didn't. Loaded her right to the muzzle. Drink? Sure I'll have a drink."

Dixie poured out a stiff one, downed it, and wiped his gray whiskers.

"Lord—think of that! Kellan with his gun hand ruint! And that other mitt of his'n useless, too, as far as gun work is concerned. Ever hear of a gunman that couldn't shoot a gun?—well, that's Kellan." Dixie looked around, a new marveling light appearing in his spaniel's eyes.

"Why, a thing like that is worse than death to a gunman. I could walk right up to him and spit in his eye. Anybody could. Walk right up and spit in his eye . . . "

VIGILANTE

H. A. DeRosso

BEFORE World War II, the primary ingredient of the pulp Western story was, as Max Brand once said, "action, action, action." Everything else was subordinate. And the tone of the story had to be lively, upbeat, so as to provide a happy (or at least a not unhappy) ending; the bleak fictional landscape of Walter Van Tilburg Clark's The Oxbow Incident, *for example, was anathema to pulp editors in those years. But following the war, readers and editors alike began to expand their horizons, to permit an occasional story such as "Vigilante" to appear among the traditional fare. A brooding, "literary" character study set during Montana's turbulent vigilante era, it is a tale that could not have been published in any Western pulp before or during the war; and at that, when it appeared in* New Western *in 1948 it was given the old-fashioned and garish title of "Swing Your Pardner High!" to create an illusion of standard horse opera. Some readers must have been* very *surprised when they read it.*

H. A. DeRosso (1917–1962) began writing while in high school in 1935, but it was not until six years later, after 79 rejected stories, that he made his first professional sale to Western Story—*something of a monument to perseverance. During his twenty-year career he published well over 200 stories, most of them Westerns; and six Western novels, the best of which are* .44 *(1953),* End of the Gun *(1955), and* The Dark Brand *(1963). Much of his fiction portrays the darker side of human relationships without softening or apology. The motives of his heroes are usually mixed and their victories, if indeed they do triumph (a good many do not even survive), are almost always bittersweet. These unusual qualities are clearly in evidence in "Vigilante."*

Bill Leahy brought the word. "The Committee's meeting tonight, John."

John Weidler set down his newspaper and removed his spectacles. "Childress?" he asked.

"Yes."

Weidler carefully placed his spectacles in their case and cast a slight smile at his wife. He was glad that the two children were outside. He could hear their calls and laughter as they played in the backyard. John Weidler placed a hand momentarily on Martha's shoulder, then followed Leahy outside.

The evening air carried a crisp coolness and Weidler buttoned his jacket. They were silent as they walked along, the rasp of their shoe leather on the hard-packed ground the only sound.

Finally Weidler said, "It's come to a head this time."

Leahy nodded. He was a big man with a wide face and a violent redness to his features. For all his weight his step was light and soft—the tread of a stalking cat.

"He has asked for it," said Leahy heavily. "Matt Childress raised hell last night. Shot up half a dozen places, broke the windows of the Mercantile. When the marshal tried to arrest him this morning, Matt tore up the writ and threw it in the marshal's face. Matt sure did go and ask for it."

They walked along in the quickly gathering twilight. Virginia City was unnaturally quiet—such a quiet that it had never known. A far call from the Virginia City of a year ago—the Virginia City of Henry Plummer and the Innocents.

Weidler kept envisioning the old Virginia City that had been a tent city with its gambling houses and saloons and its roughly-clothed, roistering miners and thieving, murdering Innocents. Full of wild, primitive laughter and full of sudden death.

A year had wrought a lot of changes in Virginia City. The tents were gone, replaced by frame buildings, though the saloons and gambling houses remained. It was a changed

Virginia City with its muted laughter and vibrant life. A place where a man could settle down and raise a family. And the Vigilantes had made it so.

"What's the word from Nevada?" Weidler asked.

"Hang him," Leahy said bluntly.

"That will be going kind of far," murmured Weidler, a sudden coldness gripping him. He was a short, stocky man in his early thirties and there was the appearance of great strength in his arms and shoulders. He had a rather plain face with a blunt jaw and there was the hint of the bulldog in his features and in his bearing. He looked like a cold man.

"It's up to the Committee," said Leahy.

"This is going to be hard, Bill. Matt was one of us. He's not a bad sort when he's sober. Drunk, he's a wild man. We've warned him time and again, but it hasn't done any good."

"He's been bragging that the Vigilantes are through."

"We'll see about that."

"Matt has friends. They'll put up a fuss. You can bet on Tom Kincaid putting up for Matt."

"Yes, Tom will do that. The hell of it is—Tom is our friend, too."

"So is Matt Childress."

They came to Day & Miller's store, where the Vigilante meeting was to be held. Miners crowded in front of the store and they all had rifles but they were a quiet, somber lot. Weidler and Leahy nodded to a few of them and entered the store.

Two kerosene lamps had been lit and their shadowy, wavering light left heavy patches of black shadow in the corners and on the far walls. About twenty men were waiting. They were all morose and quiet, carrying about them a nervous silence as though wanting everything over with as soon as possible.

One of the men spoke, "I just saw Childress. Warned him to leave town. He laughed and said the Vigilantes are played out. That they won't dare hang a man for shooting up the town."

Every man's glance was on Weidler. He'd been one of the early organizers of the Vigilantes and he'd placed the noose around George Ives's neck when that first member of the Innocents had been executed. The men were very silent now, only the scraping of their boots when they shifted their weight marring the stillness. Weidler knew they were awaiting his words.

They would put much weight to what he'd say, Weidler realized. They had always looked to him for leadership and he had never failed them. But this time things were different. Matt Childress was a friend, not a thieving, murdering outlaw. His only fault lay in his inability to hold liquor.

Weidler felt the cold sweat stand out on the back of his neck. This was not going to be easy.

"There's not much to say," Weidler said tonelessly. "You all know Matt Childress's record. He's not at all bad when sober. He has no criminal record. But this is not the first time that he has shot up the town, destroyed property and endangered the lives of citizens.

"And it is not the first time he has laughed at and ignored the law. He is a bad example. If he keeps on getting away with it, there will be others to follow his ways. He can't be reformed."

He paused a while, searching his mind for more to say. He could go on and list Matt Childress's good points. In all fairness Matt had that much coming, but the time for loyalty and sentiment was past, Weidler told himself. He had to think of what Childress meant to Virginia City, not what he meant to John Weidler.

At length he went on. "Matt Childress is your friend—and my friend. But that should not prejudice our decision. Nevada has sent word that Matt Childress should hang and that is the voice of six hundred miners. Now that decision is up to us—the Executive Committee. We all want Virginia

City and Montana Territory to be a law-abiding place where honest men can live in peace and security.

"You will vote 'Aye' or 'Nay'."

It was Bill Leahy who broke the silence, saying, "Aye." One by one the others echoed Leahy's vote and the matter was done. Leahy walked behind the counter and took down a rope.

They acted quickly, anxious to get a distasteful thing done and out of the way. John Weidler led them out of Day & Miller's store. The group of armed miners were still there. Silent. Waiting. Some of them had lighted torches.

Weidler read their unspoken query and he bobbed his head in a wordless answer. They fell in behind the Committee.

Matt Childress was in Fielding's saloon, standing at the bar with Tom Kincaid at his side. Childress's face went white and he seemed to shrink a little when he spied Weidler, but only for a moment. Childress squared his shoulders and there was a tight smile on his pale lips as he waited for the Vigilantes to speak.

Kincaid had tensed, his face taking on the color of his red hair. Heat came to his eyes. They were friends, these men. They'd ridden through storm and cold to bring summary justice to the cutthroat Innocents. They'd worked side by side—John Weidler, Matt Childress, Bill Leahy, Tom Kincaid.

"We've come for you, Matt," said Weidler.

"This is a hell of a joke to play on a man, John." Childress's voice trembled a little.

"It's no joke, Matt."

Tom Kincaid pushed forward, facing Weidler. "Are you really going through with it, John?"

"Yes."

Kincaid's face worked and it seemed as though he was going to unloose a torrent of words. But no sounds came, although his eyes distended and a sneer curled his lips. His eyes were flat and ice-cold.

Childress's thick face was very white now. "You can't mean hanging," he said, forcing a quavering laugh. "I know I'm in the wrong and I'm damned sorry. I swear before God it won't happen again. I got something coming. Banishment, maybe—but not hanging!"

Slowly, wishing that it could be otherwise, John Weidler shook his head. He was thankful that he was a reticent man who could hide his emotions behind a cold exterior, or he could never have endured watching the life going out from Matt Childress's eyes and the way he leaned against the bar as though he could not stand alone.

"You'll give me a little time then?" Childress asked dully. "A little time to put my affairs in order and to write a few letters? And to see my wife?"

"You have an hour," said Weidler.

"But an hour isn't enough! She can't make it here in that time."

"One hour," said John Weidler, turning away.

They had taken Matt Childress to one of the back rooms of Fielding's saloon where the doomed man had been supplied with pen and paper. Weidler was outside in the cold darkness, leaning against the front of the saloon. There was a cold cigar in Weidler's mouth but he kept drawing on it as if unaware that it had died.

Presently Wayne Dunning came up. He was a young man who clerked in Day & Miller's store. "They've sent a rider for Elizabeth Childress. As soon as the meeting was over and the verdict known, the rider took out for Childress's place. His wife will sure raise hell if she gets here before the execution."

"A woman's tears have a way of moving a man," said Weidler, frowning. "Tears once saved Hayes Lyons and Buck Stinson and Ned Ray from the noose and left them free to murder and rob for almost a year. But she won't get here in time."

"She'll probably use Big Bay. That horse is the fastest thing around here."

"She won't make it. What bothers me is Tom Kincaid. I thought he'd take it much harder than he has. I wonder why he hasn't?"

The hour passed and Childress's guards came out of Fielding's saloon with the doomed man walking in their midst. In the torchlight Childress's face was pasty gray and his step was a trifle unsteady.

He looked at John Weidler out of wide, haunted eyes but Weidler would not meet the man's stare. Weidler led the crowd of men to the corral in back of Day & Miller's store.

The corral gate was swung open and a rope was tossed over the crossbar. A Vigilante came out of the back of the store, carrying an empty packing box which he placed underneath the dangling noose. Bill Leahy and Wayne Dunning lifted Childress up on the box.

Childress's pale face glistened with sweat and his voice was raspingly harsh. "You can't mean this! You're all just playing a joke on me. You can't really mean to hang me for what I did last night! For getting drunk and having some fun? I'm not complaining. I deserve something for always getting out of hand and causing Virginia City a lot of trouble but I don't deserve hanging.

"I ain't ever killed but one man in all my life and he asked for it. I ain't ever robbed anyone. I've always been an honest man. Banish me. Cut off my ear or my arm but don't hang me!"

Bill Leahy had climbed up on the packing box beside Childress and Leahy fitted the noose about the doomed man's neck, and then signaled that the other end of the rope be tied to a corral post.

John Weidler stood by watching, the dead cigar still between his lips. For a while he could not believe that all this was real. But the torchlight and the milling men and Matt Childress's gray face were authentic enough and Weidler suddenly wished that all this were a dream that he might brush aside and forget upon awakening.

He hardly heard Wayne Dunning who kept whispering, "We haven't much time. She'll be here soon. We haven't much time."

There was a commotion within the crowd and Tom Kincaid came bulling his way through the armed miners. His face was very red and his eyes flashed. He bulled up close to Weidler, so close that the Vigilante leader had to fall back a step.

"Call it off, John!" Kincaid ordered.

Weidler shook his head.

"So you're really going through with it," Kincaid roared. "And I held back. Thinking that you were just trying to put the fear of death in Matt. Let him know the feel of a rope around his neck and that would calm him. That's what I thought you were up to, so I held back. I didn't think you were kill-crazy."

Weidler chewed his cold cigar. "Take it easy, Tom. Take it easy."

"You'll hang Matt only over my dead body," yelled Kincaid, swinging a wild fist at Weidler. The Vigilante had been expecting the blow and he swayed his head aside and out of Kincaid's reach.

Bill Leahy came in fast and before Kincaid could try another blow Leahy had his pistol against the back of Kincaid's neck.

"Hold on, Tom," Leahy snapped.

Kincaid dropped his arms and his fists unclenched. He never took his stare off Weidler's face. When Kincaid spoke his lips curled back from his teeth as though the very words were unclean.

"You filthy, kill-crazy murderer! I always felt you had a

bad streak in you, John, but I never would own up to it because I called you friend. I felt we needed a cold man like you to put an end to Henry Plummer and the Innocents. I never thought the killing craze would worm into you until you'd hang anyone just to satisfy your filthy craving.

"We need the Vigilantes. I was one of them, and I am not ashamed of what I did. But tonight you're tearing down all the good we ever built. You're blackening the name of the Vigilantes in a way that can never be forgotten. When histories of the Vigilantes are written you'll be marked down as a kill-crazy murderer, and all those associated with you will have to carry the same black brand."

Weidler took it all in silence. He stood there stolidly, the dead cigar clamped between his teeth, meeting Tom Kincaid's hot stare. Weidler's pulse was pounding and he could feel the throb of the vein at his temple.

He knew a coldness that filled him completely, the identical coldness he'd always felt at moments like these. Kincaid's words fell as from an alien world.

"One word from you and Matt could be saved," Kincaid went on. "Had you stood up for Matt, put in a good word for him, the Committee would never have voted as it did.

"It's an evil and dark day for Montana Territory when you've taken to hanging men for minor offenses. But Matt Childress will be the first and the last. I can't save him. I know that. But I'll see to it that you'll never hang another. Mind that, John."

Weidler turned his head and his stare away from Kincaid. Matt Childress was mumbling brokenly, incoherently on the packing box. Weidler felt a weakness creeping over his will. The time had come and he had to make his choice—between Matt Childress and a Virginia City that would be quiet and still and peaceful, where a man could live and be proud of his town.

And suddenly he realized that if he hesitated much longer, he could not go through with it.

So he took the cigar from his mouth and said clearly, coldly, "Men, do your duty!"

Afterward, when Childress's lifeless body was swaying in the night wind, there came the thunderous clopping of a horse's hoofs and a rider burst into the smoky torchlight. It was a woman, and she flung herself out of the saddle before the horse had halted. She stopped short when she spied the dangling body.

Weidler was up against the corral fence with Bill Leahy and Wayne Dunning on either side of him. They all watched Elizabeth Childress. She was a tall woman with a violently beautiful face. They knew little about her except that she lived with Matt Childress and he called her his wife. She stared at Childress's body a long while, but no tears or cries came. She spoke at last, her voice choking with grief.

"Oh, the shame of it," she cried as she knelt beneath the dead man and clasped her arms around his stiffening legs. "That Matt Childress should be hanged like a common felon. Where were his friends? Why did they let this happen to him who was a better man than all of them?

"Better that someone had taken a gun and shot my Matt down. If I had been here, I'd have done that—rather than suffer him to hang!"

She seemed to notice Weidler for the first time. The woman rose slowly to her feet and she walked haltingly, stooped forward a little as if to see better. And as she came close, Weidler saw the tightness of her features and the way the cords stood out on her neck.

He expected her to speak, to burst out in an orgy of denunciations, but she only stared at him, her lips working silently. Then she went back to Childress.

Weidler spat the shredded cigar from his teeth and walked away.

He found that Martha had put the children to bed and that she had a pot of boiling coffee on the stove for him. She didn't say anything but he could feel from her silent presence that she yearned for some comforting words to say to him.

He poured the coffee with fingers that were stiffly untrembling and, looking up, he caught her eyes and smiled a little.

"You'd better go to bed," he told her. "I'm staying up a while longer."

She left the room and he was instantly sorry she had gone. It felt so empty now—empty as he was himself. All he knew was a hollow feeling within him and a vast restlessness. He went to the kitchen door and threw it open, standing full in the soft sweep of the night wind.

He stood looking off at the sky but not seeing the stars or the moon or the scattered clouds flowing along with the wind. All he saw was Matt Childress's swaying body and the loathing and hatred in Tom Kincaid's eyes.

He was standing there in the chillness of the night when Bill Leahy came again.

"What is it, Bill?"

"Tom Kincaid is after you."

"He'll get over it."

Leahy placed a big hand against the doorjamb. His breathing had calmed. "He's taken on a load of drinks. He's in a bad mind, John. He's coming over here to have it out with you."

"He's drunk. He doesn't know what he's doing."

"But he's doing it just the same."

"Why has he got it in for me?" Weidler asked savagely.

"He blames you for Matt. Says if you'd put in a good word for Matt, he'd never been hanged. There's no telling Tom otherwise. I've tried for half an hour but Tom won't listen."

"Then I'll have to try," said Weidler.

"He's got a gun, John."

Weidler shrugged. Bill Leahy came in close and slipped something into Weidler's pocket. He reached down and felt the cold metal of a revolver.

They had turned out into the street when they spied the

man coming toward them. He walked with a rolling step much like a sailor's but Weidler knew that the roll of the walk was due to too many drinks.

Kincaid had stopped, his legs planted wide. His head was thrust forward and he raised a hand and pushed his hat back from his forehead. Recognition came to him for he laughed and said:

"Well, well, if it ain't Bloody John!"

"Hello, Tom," said Weidler easily. "I'm on my way to Fielding's for a drink. Will you join me?"

"Drink, hell!" exploded Kincaid wrathfully. Then he laughed again. "I won't join you in a drink but you sure will join Matt in hell!"

He had been holding his right hand at his belt and he suddenly flung up his arm. Weidler saw moonlight flash on the polished metal of Kincaid's pistol.

"Hold it, you damn fool!" Weidler cried, rushing forward. Kincaid laughed and his cold eyes looked down the sights of his gun but his bullet was wide.

Before he could fire again, Weidler was on him.

Kincaid was bringing his weapon up again but Weidler grasped the gun, holding it away from him. Kincaid lunged, grunting, and he drove the hard toe of his boot into Weidler's shin. Weidler released his hold and as he wavered on the point of unbalance, Kincaid shoved out his leg, sending Weidler sprawling.

He rolled over quickly to find himself staring in the bore of Kincaid's weapon.

Weidler hardly realized his actions. Perhaps it was the instinct of self-preservation that prompted him to act so automatically. For the gun in his hand roared, and as Kincaid staggered, it roared again.

Kincaid made a half-turn and it looked as if he wanted to walk away when he said quite clearly, "Oh my God!" and fell.

They came running, the watching men, and they gathered around the fallen Tom Kincaid. Weidler's friends were about him, but he was heedless to their queries about his welfare. Two words stuck to his mind as he walked away. Two words hurled at him by someone looking down at dead Tom Kincaid.

"Bloody killer!"

A strange, cold loneliness settled down over Weidler. He knew that he'd never forget the double tragedy of this night. The memory of it would ever haunt him, but, looking about him, he saw that Virginia City was quiet now, a natural quiet, and that was consolation enough.

A WOLLOPIN' GOOD CHEW

Thomas Thompson

HUMOR in Western pulp fiction was generally of the broad, farcical variety. Much of it was provided by Gabby Hayes-style foils and sidekicks, and much by ethnic stereotypes; very little was subtle or situational. The pulp audience had scant patience for the more sophisticated forms of comedy. They wanted their funnybones tickled by the same type of overt zaniness the Marx Brothers and Abbott & Costello gave them on the silver screen.

Most serious Western writers eschewed the comic story for this reason. It was simply too difficult for the best ones to write down to the necessary base level. But certain ideas are irresistable, and so some talented writers did *have a fling at humor now and then. One such writer is Thomas Thompson; and "A Wollopin' Good Chew" is that* rara avis, *a funny Western tale that is neither coarse nor ridiculous, and every bit as chucklesome today as it was when it first appeared in 1948.*

California native Tommy Thompson's Western stories, whether for the pulps or for such slicks as Collier's *and* The Saturday Evening Post, *were among the best-crafted of their time. Two—"Gun Job" and "Blood on the Sun"—won back-to-back Spur Awards from the Western Writers of America as the best shorts of 1953 and 1954, respectively; these and others can be found in his collections,* They Brought Their Guns *(1953) and* Moment of Glory *(1961). Equally fine are his novels, among the most memorable of which are* Broken Valley *(1949),* The Steel Web *(1953), and* Brand of a Man *(1958). Thompson turned to TV writing in the fifties, and for many years was associated with the classic Western show "Bonanza," as scriptwriter, story consultant, and associate producer.*

It was more than Finnegan had expected. Visible from the stage road both ways, staring majestically across the golden undulating hay-filled meadows to the blue peaks beyond . . .

It seemed almost in tune with the sunrise that forced its positive golds and reds through the rift of tumbling storm clouds that had come up with the night. To put anything but an EIDERDOWN SOAP sign on a barn such as this would be sacrilege, thought Leon Finnegan the painter.

A pleasing touch of satisfying evil found its way around the sensitive soul of Finnegan as he thought of Fred Maben back there in Columbia sleeping off a big head. It had cost Finnegan ten dollars last night in an honest attempt to keep Fred Maben and his unlovely Cut Plug signs away from this barn.

It had meant that Finnegan had driven his own paint-spattered wagon half the night over bad roads in order to get here early. He breathed deeply of the morning air, rich with its promise of rain. It had been worth it. There'd be no Cut Plug mule on the graceful slopes of the Twin Butte Stage Station barn. All Finnegan had to do now was sell the idea to Jonathan Phelps.

Before turning in the lane, Finnegan permitted himself one more soul-satisfying look at the switch-back grade that lead to Strawberry. Even nature had conspired to make it beautiful.

There was the sunrise; and the conical manure piles had not yet appeared to break the gentle slope that drifted away from the square-cut windows. It was a thing of beauty a man could dwell on, but Finnegan was forced back to the harsher realities of life, for coming down the lane was the hulking form of Jonathan Phelps on an equally hulking horse.

Finnegan got that vacant feeling in the pit of his stomach. Jonathan Phelps affected him that way. Maybe it was the size of him—maybe only what men said about him. Finnegan didn't know. The size maybe.

It was reputed to be six-foot-two any way you measured,

but eyeing him now Finnegan figured Phelps might fall a little short of that across the shoulders. As for what men said . . . Well, they said lots of things.

In the saloons around Columbia men liked to sink their faces in the suds of locally made beer and tell pridefully of how Jonathan Phelps had broken a man's neck with his bare hands. When they tired of that they would speak reverently of how Jonathan Phelps had beaten the heads of two miners together until the unfortunate men were gibbering idiots for the remainder of their lives. At this point some one would always look up and say, "Seen 'em myself."

Then the men would leer at each other with protruding eyes and foam-soaked mustaches and say, "Did you ever hear of road agents on the Columbia-Strawberry road?" And in answer to their own question they would say, "Ha!"

And Leon Finnegan, the sign painter, had to admit it was true. Not even Miguel Torres had ever tried to rob a gold-laden Strawberry-Columbia stage.

That point in itself was enough to give a man all the reputation he'd ever need to carry him through a natural span of life, for the wily Miguel Torres had taken a sizeable sample of practically every gold shipment that had ever moved anyplace between Los Angeles and Yreka.

But Jonathan Phelps had even more than that to recommend him, and Finnegan was vividly conscious of it as the big man stopped, his feet thrust deep in the stirrups, the width of him taking up the entire saddle and more.

The big man opened his mouth and a sound came out. With a lesser man it might have been a questioning "Well?" But with Jonathan Phelps it was a bellowing roar that ignited a long dead spark of life in Leon Finnegan's two horses. They reared and plunged against the harness and Finnegan had his hands full for a second getting them back in shape. The display seemed pleasing to Jonathan Phelps.

Finnegan wrapped the lines around the brake, tugged the

contour of his vest in place, smoothed his mustache with the flat of a fingernail, doffed his hard hat, and said, "Good morning Mr. Phelps. Beautiful morning, isn't it?"

"Never mind the sassafras," roared Jonathan Phelps. "Get down to cases, man."

"You have a barn yonder," said Finnegan, waving his hand. "The most magnificent barn ever to grace California's landscape. Here in this wagon of mine I have the stain and the pigments to make that barn impervious to the elements until the end of time."

Finnegan cocked his head at the lowering clouds, sniffed deeply of the fragrant air, and rubbed the balls of his thumb and forefinger together. "Feels like rain, too," he said.

"Get on with your say, man," said Jonathan Phelps, a hint of interest in his eyes. Not even Jonathan Phelps could pass up a chance at a free paint job on a barn. "What kind of signs you paint?"

Finnegan had introduced himself and was halfway through with his well-rehearsed spiel on Eiderdown Soap when he heard the voice of Jonathan Phelps, twice as shocking now for the softness of it. The big man said, "By any chance did you paint the sign on the side of Madame O'Brion's Millinery Salon there in town?"

Finnegan beamed. To Finnegan there had never been another piece of art like the one on the side of Madame O'Brion's Millinery Salon. The day he painted that he had been inspired. The six-foot letters in Eiderdown and Soap had an old English gracefulness about them. Entwining tendrils softened the corners of the otherwise oblong offering.

By closing his eyes slightly Finnegan could still see the myriad bubbles that floated up from the enticing white cake. Bubbles with a personality, each one cross-hatched with bright-colored little windows representing the prismatic light of the sun.

The only thing unlovely about that sign was the well-known advertising slogan, TAKES TO WATER LIKE A DUCK. That sign was the sort of thing that belonged on the roof of the Twin Buttes Stage Station barn. Finnegan blew on his nails and said, "You may consider that an example of my work. Yes."

Jonathan Phelps's voice was still soft. He said, "Would you tell me something, Mr. Finnegan?"

"Gladly," said Finnegan, rubbing his nails on his vest.

"Just what is the animal in that sign, Mr. Finnegan?" said Jonathan Phelps softly. "A duck that's had its neck stretched out or a swan that's had its head beat in?" There was nothing soft about his voice now.

"Now jest a derned minute," said Finnegan. "That happens to be—"

"Get your riggin' out of my lane," roared Jonathan Phelps. "Take it up to the house and turn it around and head back to your bubbles. I got other ideas about what I want on my barn!"

"For example?" said Finnegan, his voice matching the volume of Jonathan Phelps.

"For example, a mule like is on Mulrooney's saloon," said Jonathan Phelps. "That's what for example."

Finnegan felt all the blood draining out of his cheeks. His eyes rolled toward that beautiful barn with the most natural expanse of roof man had ever created for an Eiderdown Soap sign. He thought of the inartistic Mr. Fred Maben and his unesthetic mule and there was a pleading supplication in his voice when he said, "Not that, Mr. Phelps. Not that!"

"And why not?" said Jonathan Phelps. "Something you can see fer a good way off and something that'll turn the rain. And besides . . ." He nudged his horse against Finnegan's wagon, worked his jaws for a pair of seconds, and spat lustily. "Besides," he said, "it's a dern good product."

With that he pushed his way past the wagon, saying, "Don't

take up no more of my time, Mr. Finnegan. It's clabberin' up to rain, I got four men waitin' and a whole dern field full of hay to get in. Good day, Mr. Finnegan!"

Finnegan was not a man who gave up easily, but there was something a little awe-inspiring about Jonathan Phelps, to say the least. Finnegan hadn't quite reached a decision as to how he would handle the situation when he pulled the wagon up under the wide spreading chinaberry trees that stood in front of the hulking ranch house.

Mr. Finnegan's artistic soul told him he should drive down the lane, never bothering to look back at the habitation of one as uncouth as Jonathan Phelps. But the same soul wistfully told him that he would never again in his life see such a beautiful spot for an Eiderdown Soap sign as the roof of that new barn.

Mr. Finnegan's more practical soul told him that if he stayed very long he was apt to get his head mashed in. But regardless, he took his time about turning the wagon, watching the scatter of chickens walk with that peculiar cawing tiptoeing sidewise stance a chicken assumes when the air is still and the rain is near.

Over by the corral where the fresh stage team waited, a peacock spread its fan and gave a piercing gawking cry that was suddenly everywhere in the flat dead air. Finnegan did not like the sound of a peacock. Nor did he like the sound that immediately followed it. Finnegan could not stand to hear a woman cry.

He didn't really mean to look, but they were standing there so boldly, just beyond the trunk of that chinaberry tree. The young man staring dismally into nothing, the young girl with her head on the young man's chest.

At regular intervals her shoulders would give three little hops followed by an afterbeat of two audible sobs. The soul of Mr. Finnegan was touched. Then the girl drew back a little, beat the young man on the chest with both her clenched fists, and said, "You empty-headed idiot, why don't you say something?"

The young man said something. It sounded like "Dah."

Finnegan paused with one foot on the hub of the off-wheel of the wagon and the other on the ground. It was at the precise moment that the peacock decided to make another unearthly sound.

Finnegan's team did not like peacocks any more than Finnegan did. The horses made a sudden move to the left. Finnegan's foot slipped off the hub and he was there in the dust of the yard, no longer hidden by the bulk of his wagon with its paint-stained ladders and its pigment-slick scaffolding.

He got up slowly, bowed, took off his hard hat and brushed the dust from his clothes with it. He smiled again and said, "Good morning. Nice morning, isn't it?"

The girl with the tear-stained face and the boy with the vacant eyes looked at him but they said nothing. Finnegan looked back and said the same. The girl was beautiful in a number of ways. She had exactly the right amount of everything in exactly the right places. She had get-up-and-go in her eyes and linger-awhile on her lips. A perky nose and a determined chin and a general yielding softness.

Finnegan realized suddenly that had he been twenty years younger he would have at this moment been able to do nothing more than say, "Dah." The young man didn't look so silly after all, he thought.

In fact, the young fellow had a lot of rugged manhood about him. He was tall; he was broad; there were hard balls of muscle that kept rolling around at the end of his jaw bone and he had a chin that looked like it had been shaped from hot metal with a hammer.

The only thing wrong with him was that his mouth was slightly open and eyes that could have been unusually nice were fogged by a gaze that was totally blank. But Leon Finnegan smiled softly. His soul told him that anybody who could look that completely stupid at this hour of the morning was desperately in love.

The tears in the eyes of the girl told Finnegan that this love was not one-sided. It also told him that things were not running smoothly. For some reason he thought of that bellowing, hulking man who had come riding down the lane on an equally hulking horse. He looked again at the girl, founded a family resemblance that was no detriment. That was all he needed.

In a handful of understanding minutes Finnegan had won the confidence of Barbara Phelps and a vacant-eyed Cornelius Regan who preferred to be called Neil. He had learned too that sign-painting was not the only thing about which Jonathan Phelps had ideas.

As soon as the Strawberry stage arrived and the switch in teams was made, Mr. Cornelius Regan was to be an ex-employee of the Twin Butte Stage Station. Like Finnegan he had been advised not to tarry.

Finnegan catalogued the qualifications of Cornelius Regan and again noted the obvious enticements of Barbara Phelps. He said, "But, look here—"

"Daddy likes a man who talks back to him!" wailed Barbara Phelps by way of explanation.

Cornelius Regan confirmed that. He said, "Dah." Young Regan had reached the stage in his love life where the world is liquid and the stars do not leave with the sunrise.

It would take a great shock to put this young man back into normal action, Finnegan saw. He was sure of his decision, but he didn't expect the shock to materialize so soon. It came up the lane. It came in the form of five mounted men—four in a tight block, one in the lead. They were the most murderous-looking men Finnegan had ever seen in his life.

The girl took one look at them and threw herself into the arms of Cornelius Regan. Regan smiled vacantly and tightened his arms around her. He seemed happy. Finnegan kept making dry clacking sounds with his store teeth until the band of horsemen were within ten feet, had drawn their six-shooters, cocked them, and pointed them unerringly at Finnegan's head.

Then the cutthroat who rode in the lead said, "This will all be very simple. There is to be no argument. As you all know well, I, Miguel Torres, do not like to have people talk back."

The bandit chief smiled, smacked the palm of his left hand against the wide Spanish horn of his saddle, looked first at the lovers, and said, "You. In the house." Then at Finnegan and said, "You. Go paint the sign."

Finnegan said, "But, but—"

Miguel Torres got off his horse. He got off slowly. He walked slowly, followed by his loud musical clanking of his huge roweled spurs. He walked up to Mr. Finnegan and he took Mr. Finnegan by the throat. He spoke very softly.

"Perhaps you do not understand," said Miguel Torres patiently. "I will tell you once. For six months now, I, Miguel Torres, have waited for this day. The rain is coming, so Jonathan Phelps and his men are fighting time to get the hay in.

"There is but one man here to change the stage horses. The stage is coming and there is gold on that stage. It is the way Miguel Torres plans things. I do not plan you should come today to paint the barn. But you are here. Jonathan Phelps can see the barn from the hay field and he is a hard man.

"If he sees you are not doing your work he will come to find out why. I do not want Mr. Phelps and his men to come here today." He momentarily tightened his grip around Finnegan's throat, released him quickly, and drew a forefinger across Finnegan's fluttering Adam's apple. He smiled and said, "Go paint the barn!"

Finnegan hurried to comply, and as he was leaving he

heard Miguel Torres say suggestively, "You are beautiful. I could not believe a pig like Jonathan Phelps could have such a beautiful daughter. Come a little closer."

Finnegan heard Cornelius Regan make a sound that did not sound like "Dah." He turned in time to see the young man land a blow that knocked all suggestiveness out of the bandit chief—who landed six feet away from Barbara Phelps.

Finnegan also saw three or four gun barrels land with a rather loud crunch on Regan's head. And as Finnegan turned to get his paints and brushes he saw them drag Cornelius Regan into the house, heels first.

Leon Finnegan was sick. He thought nothing could make him sicker. Then he heard a familiar clattering sound and looked up. There in the lane, coming too fast for his own good, was Fred Maben and his Cut Plug sign-painting wagon.

Finnegan hid his eyes while Miguel Torres and his men handled Mr. Fred Maben. Within five minutes the Cut Plug painter was side by side with Finnegan, opening buckets, leaning ladders, and rigging scaffolding. Mr. Maben's blood-shot eyes kept rolling like marbles and his walrus mustache kept humping up and down. Miguel Torres had said that Mr. Fred Maben should assist Mr. Finnegan. Neither Mr. Finnegan nor Mr. Maben wished to argue the point.

Fred Maben had one stock argument to offer in defense of his art. He'd roll his product in his jowls, take a wollopin' good spit at any moving target, and say, "Maybe she ain't pretty fer nice, but she's hell fer strong and she'll keep yore roof from leakin'."

And somehow, with an unimaginative argument like that, Fred Maben got too many jobs to do. It had gotten to the point where Finnegan didn't like Fred Maben.

Fred Maben, Finnegan often thought, was a lot like the

signs he painted. Solid and practical, but wholly unlovely. The towering unimaginative letters of his Mule's Heel Cut Plug sign were always done in vivid yellow. The mule was always northbound, looking back over its shoulder, if a mule could do such a thing, exposing its unlovely south end and its unesthetic rear feet.

Sort of flowing off the mule's heels was the immodest proclamation which said, A WOLLOPIN' GOOD CHEW. The sign was much like the man who painted it.

But the presence of death has a way of drawing men together when nothing else will. Fred Maben's bloodshot eyes were not altogether forgiving, and his breath still held an aroma reminiscent of the way Finnegan had tried to keep his competitor away from Jonathan Phelps's new barn, but the presence of death knotted the tie, nevertheless.

They worked like a team setting their ladders, rigging their scaffolds, and stirring their paint. Both men had slipped on coveralls and painter's caps, and as they left the scaffold and started up the long slope of the barn, buckets and brushes in hand, they even looked alike.

Together they turned and looked back, perhaps for the last time. Down at the end of the lane, stretching out to the rimming cup of the hills, was the hay field where Jonathan Phelps and his four helpers worked feverishly to get the wind-rowed hay into shocks and the shocks into a bulging roofed-over stack at the far edge of the meadow.

Beyond the house, hidden from view, were the horses of Miguel Torres's bandits. Far up on the shoulder of the hill zig-zagged the dusty white chalk line of road that would bring the gold-laden stage down to its doom. It was not an inspiring picture.

Finnegan swallowed his pride, looked at his competitor, and said, "What are we going to do?"

Fred Maben chewed his cud thoughtfully and laid a deep brown stripe down the slope of the split shake roof. He said,

"I've no idea what a lout like you might be fixin' to do. Me, I'm a practical man. I sees a situation and I sizes it up."

He focused his eyes down his prominent nose, blew through his mustache, and tossed his head toward the men in the hay field. "You, I suppose," he said, "will be thinking about ducks. Me, I figger on paintin' 'HELP' clean across the top of this barn!"

The simplicity of it struck Mr. Finnegan hard. It was the sort of thing he would never have thought of himself. More likely the real issue at hand would have been too clouded by his concern over whether Cornelius Regan would ever get the stars out of his eyes in time to see that the girl was in love with him too.

But now that Fred Maben had come up with such a simple solution he felt he owed a lot to the great man. He said, "Fred, that's wonderful. I want you to know I feel bad about last night, old friend. And there's something else. . . ."

A soft voice from below floated its precise English up to them. It said, "Gentlemen, I feel I should tell you to be exceedingly careful what you paint. I can read."

They looked down and there, leaning against Finnegan's wagon, was a bright-colored blanket. There was an evil-looking head with a sombrero sticking through the blanket. There was also a rifle that was tilted toward the two painters on the roof.

Fred Maben said, "Oh."

Finnegan said, "Bright idea you had, Mr. Maben. Very bright indeed."

Fred Maben was a practical man. After thinking it over for some time he said, "Finnegan, it's been nice knowing you. I'd been lonesome without you to fight with." He offered his hand.

Finnegan took the hand and he felt a little tight lump in his throat. He said, "You make it sound so final."

Fred Maben said, "I'm a practical man. I'm a man who puts everything he has into one idea. I risk it all on a flip of pitch and toss. That's the kind of a man I am. It is final."

Finnegan said, "But we have got to put a stop to this nonsense. I don't want to die."

Fred Maben said, "I've led a full life." He looked at Finnegan. "There's a few things I want to confess before I go," he said. His eyes were doleful. He said, "Finnegan, it was me that put the molasses in your linseed oil."

Finnegan couldn't find it in his heart to hold it against the man. He said, "It's all right. Now."

"But I feel mighty low down about it," Fred Maben said.

"You mustn't," said Finnegan.

"But I do," said the practical-minded Fred Maben.

The gentle soul of Leon Finnegan rebelled at seeing such contrite remorse. He said, "Would it cheer you up any if you knew that Jonathan Phelps had planned on giving you the job of painting this barn?"

"It would help if I knew that," admitted Fred Maben.

"It's the truth," said Finnegan. "He told me so himself. He doesn't like my duck. Hates it, in fact. He likes your mule. That's what he wants on the roof of his barn."

The sudden meshing of the two minds was audible. Fred Maben's voice was a hoarse whisper. "Then if Jonathan Phelps should look up and see a duck on his roof—"

"He wouldn't like it," said the oggle-eyed Leon Finnegan.

They wasted no more time. They set to work, faster than sign painters had ever worked before. Fred Maben even whistled and sang a little as he stodgily roughed out the curling tail feathers of the famous soap-selling drake. It made Leon Finnegan feel all warm and wiggly inside. He knew *he* couldn't whistle and sing while painting a mule.

He said, "Maben, you're a great man, really. I mean after all I've done to you—trying to trick you out of this job and all. To have you pitch in and even be happy helping me at my work." He looked sidewise as Fred Maben, unable to conceal the satisfaction on his face. "You realize, of course, that after the great service this duck is going to render it will naturally remain on this roof."

Fred Maben said, "I figger you don't know the mind of Jonathan Phelps, Finnegan. I was jest cipherin' out in my mind how much extra my company should give me when it comes time for me to paint out this blasted duck of yours and put on the beautiful mule Jonathan Phelps so rightly wants."

Given a little time Leon Finnegan could have made a proper and fitting answer. But time was a thing of which there was little. They heard the faint halloo and the rattle of wheels reaching all this way on the moist air.

And looking up toward the notch that nicked the shoulder of the hill they could see the plume of dust that told of the gold-laden Strawberry stage starting down the many switch-backs toward the waiting guns of Miguel Torres. Leon Finnegan looked at Fred Maben, and Fred Maben looked at Leon Finnegan. There was a duck to be painted in a hurry.

It was a big duck. It took up most of the upper slope of the barn. It had a black head and a multicolored body. There was some red and some yellow and an abundance of green. It was lumpy in spots as if perhaps it had been eating rocks. But it was a duck, and it was noticeable, and from time to time Finnegan and Fred Maben would stand aside and wave their arms a bit to make the duck even more noticeable from the hay field.

And in time it was noticeable and a cloud of dust from the hay field raced a cloud of dust from the lower switch-backs toward the big barn there at the station. The day was saved.

Jonathan Phelps and his hard-bitten crew were coming to the rescue. Finnegan strutted proudly there on the roof of the barn. His duck would be immortal. And then he saw the color drain out of the face of that practical man Fred Maben. He looked and saw the trouble.

The dust cloud from the hay field had beaten the dust cloud from the switch-backs all right, but it would do little good. Standing up in his stirrups, howling great threats at his sorrel mare, was Jonathan Phelps. There was no one else. He hadn't brought his hard-bitten crew with him. He had come alone.

Defeat drained the life from Finnegan and Maben. They sat down near their partially finished duck and awaited the coming of death. The bellowing mouthings of Jonathan Phelps jerked them back to their feet. The least they could do was warn the man that he was about to die.

But things started happening too fast for thought. There was a crackle of gunfire from the big house. Jonathan Phelps's hat went sailing off into the air and Jonathan Phelps's wild-eyed mare went sailing off without Jonathan Phelps.

Which left the big man standing in the middle of the lane, bellowing and roaring, jumping high and landing hard, dodging first one way and then the other as the little spumes of dust spurted up around his feet.

There was a howl of pain from the house as if someone had just lost a finger. A door slammed and looking that way Finnegan saw Barbara Phelps, her skirts gathered around her knees, tearing across the hard-packed yard toward the barn.

Finnegan went into action. He scooted down toward the wide overhanging eaves of the barn, took a measuring look at the blanket-covered rifleman squatting there below him, aimed carefully, and dropped his paint bucket neatly over the man's head.

Then he slid down the ladder, missing every rung, got his arms around Barbara Phelps, and dragged her into the shelter of the barn, just as Fred Maben, following suit, came diving in through one of the square windows.

Barbara didn't even seem to notice that her father was trying vainly to hide behind a fence post. She tried to pull out of Finnegan's grasp. She sobbed, "Neil's in there! He beat two of them over the head but they knocked him down. Now he's staggering around like he's in a daze!"

"Again?" said Finnegan. And an idea struck him. He said, "Start screaming, girl."

She said, "What?"

He said, "Loud."

She didn't argue. She screamed. She had inherited some of the lung power of her father. Her scream rattled against Finnegan's eardrums. It was louder even than the squeal of the brakes on the stage that rocked to a dust-choked stop there in front of the barn.

"That should do it," said Finnegan.

There was a horrible racket from the house then. After a series of sounds not unlike the crunching of bones, Cornelius Regan appeared in the front door. He had a minimum of clothes and a maximum of six-shooters. He was making rumbling sounds deep in his throat.

Suddenly, from out a side window, came Miguel Torres and one of his henchmen. They saw Cornelius Regan standing there, gave a yell of terror, and started to run in the other direction. But Regan overtook them. He made a flying tackle, brought them down, picked them up by the scruff of the neck, and banged their heads together loudly. Then he came stalking toward the barn.

He saw Barbara and he got that glazed look in his eyes. Finnegan said, "No! No!" and he pointed frantically toward where Jonathan Phelps, out from behind his fence post now, was bellowing orders to the stage driver, the shotgun guard, and the two well-armed passengers. The glazed look left the eyes of Cornelius Regan.

He turned around, walked up to Jonathan Phelps, laced his fingers through the big man's collar, shook him until his jowls made a slapping sound, then said, "I love your daughter, sir. Hear that? I'm going to marry her, sir. You got anything to say about it—sir?"

Jonathan Phelps's voice was shaky as he tried unsuccessfully to wriggle free of the iron-bound grasp. He said, "Welcome into the family, son!"

Cornelius Regan released his hold, dusted his hands, and come toward the barn. He looked in and he saw Barbara standing there. He said, "Come here, you!"

She said, "Yes, Cornelius."

So the day passed and the evening came quietly. Fred Maben, being a practical man, realized that over-excitement, shock, and the effects of a too-strenuous night called for some stabilizing influence. He found it there in the brown bottle under the seat of his wagon. Finnegan was not a man to argue such things.

First they told Jonathan Phelps he'd take what they gave him in the way of a paint job and like it. Then, together, throughout the day, they worked side by side on both the sign and the bottle. It was a happy day. The soul of Leon Finnegan rejoiced at having someone with whom he could discuss art. There was a faraway look in his eyes when he looked at his erstswhile competitor and said, "Van Dyke's *Blue Boy*. Ah, Fred Maben. There's a painting for you!"

"Michelangelo's *Blue Boy*," corrected Fred Maben.

"Of course," said Finnegan. "Always get 'em mixed up." He was surprised and pleased to find out how much Fred Maben knew about art.

And with evening came a rift in the clouds and a gold splash of sunlight. Fred Maben and Finnegan leaned together there at the edge of the hay meadow.

Near them, outlined against the rim of mountains and the sunset, stood Barbara Phelps and Cornelius Regan. Barbara raised her face, her eyes shining. Her voice was husky. She said, "My knight in shining armor. You were wonderful, Cornelius. Tell me, what went through your mind when you heard my scream?"

Cornelius Regan gave a straight and modest answer. He said, "Dah."

But he'd get over it, Finnegan knew. It would be all right.

The world was all right. There were tears in his eyes as he looked at the sign spread there on the beautiful expanse of the Twin Butte Stage Station barn.

On the upper slope of the barn was a duck that in some ways resembled a mule. And on the lower slope of the barn there was a mule that in some ways resembled a duck. Near the soap-selling mallard was the famous Eiderdown slogan, TAKES TO WATER LIKE A DUCK.

And running diagonally, from the lower corner of the barn to the upper peak, cutting just over the Cut Plug Mule's head, were the huge letters of the compromise between Fred Maben and Finnegan.

Finnegan felt the sweet milk of brotherhood and the warm glow of Maben's bottle within him as he read the words:

> WHILE TAKING YOUR BATH,
> TRY MULE'S HEEL CUT PLUG.
> A WOLLOPIN' GOOD CHEW.

CHIVAREE

Frank Bonham

INDIANS, *blacks, Mexicans, and other minorities and for-eigners received rough treatment in the early Western pulps, as they did in other forms of popular literature during the first forty-odd years of this century. If ethnic characters weren't portrayed as villains, or dragged into stories for dubious comic relief, they were all too often shown as inferiors—and almost always made to act in stereotypical fashion and to speak in dreadful dialect. The grim years of World War II, the new awareness and compassion that came out of that intense time of global strife, put an end to the worst offenses and helped bring about a more realistic and honest depiction of ethnic groups. It is even possible to find, in the Western pulps of the postwar years, an occasional story which deals intelligently with race relations in the Old West. "Chivaree," from a 1951 issue of* Star Western, *is one such story.*

Its author, Frank Bonham, was a mainstay in the Western pulps of the period; he published stories in all the frontline magazines from 1941 to the early fifties, when he graduated to such slicks as The Saturday Evening Post. *Eminent among his score of Western novels are* Lost Stage Valley *(1948),* Snaketrack *(1952),* Cast a Long Shadow *(1964), and* Break for the Border *(1980); the last-named title is particu-larly noteworthy for its feminist heroine, a practicing attorney. Bonham is also well-known for his juvenile novels, one of which—*Durango Street *(1965)—received numerous acco-lades and was a young-adult bestseller. In addition to his fiction, he contributed scripts to "Tales of Wells Fargo," "Death Valley Days," and other Western TV shows in the fifties and sixties.*

In the dark cabin Jim felt Nettie's body start and turn toward him. Her Injun blood, he reckoned—rousing on a sound no louder than the whicker of a horse. He held her tightly with one arm while he groped beside the bed for his rifle.

"Stay right here, Nettie," he whispered. "Keep the blankets about you."

"Jim! Jim!" she whispered. "What is it?" She had seen his bare arm hunting the rifle.

"Don't know," Jim Croft grunted, piling out into his boots and heaping the blankets on her. There was no telling what—but blankets would sometimes turn a bullet.

In his nightgown—which Nettie had made him and he had to wear—he slipped to the window. He had hardly reached it when the gunfire let loose. The bullets came in a slogging rhythm against the mud wall under the eaves. It was a shattering thing; but Jim understood, now, and was reassured.

He let the bullets run out; then he called to his wife: "Chivaree! Dress quick and rustle all the cups you can."

There was a blood-chilling sound, ripped through with a wild coyote yelling. There was some grunting, too—all the sounds which passed for Indian. He wondered if Nettie got it. If she didn't get it, Reuben Lightfoot—and the crowd he had brought along for the fun—would make it plain enough.

Again the guns blasted at the cabin; hoofs thudded in the corral and the chickens were squawking. Nettie came to him, pressing fearfully against his side. Her dark hair hung in two long braids over her shoulders. Her breast was soft against his arm, and Jim wanted poignantly to make it all smooth and easy for her, to keep her pride as shining as her eyes.

"What will they do, Jim?"

"Just horse around a bit. Don't let on you're scairt. But don't take anything from Rube Lightfoot, either. The others will be all right, unless—"

He watched her pull her flowered calico gown down over her nightdress. This dark-eyed wife of his—he loved her so much it was hard to bear. Nights, he couldn't squeeze her close enough; days, he'd make chores to take him back to the cabin. They were singing-happy, but inside they had both been waiting for the thing that would determine whether they would be neighbors or outlanders . . . whether a squawman and his half-breed wife would be accepted in this recently Indian country. And now Rube Lightfoot had brought it to them.

Jim opened the door. "When you lobos get done howling at the moon, come in and wet your whistles!" he shouted.

The gobbling and firing ended. Lightfoot's rainbarrel bass rumbled. "Well, she ain't scalped him yit, evidentally!"

Out of the sagebrush tromped a dozen men. Boots scuffing, smelling of man-sweat and horse-sweat, unshaven and brazen-eyed, they crowded into the cabin. On the table, Nettie Croft had placed a jug of corn whiskey and all the vessels which could pass for cups, including two small pottery pans.

"Missus Croft," Lightfoot said, "you set a mighty fine table." He took one of the pottery vessels.

The other men crowded in to the whiskey, cowpunchers who worked for Reuben Lightfoot and small ranchers like Jim. Lightfoot said, tossing a hand at the rumpled cot, "I see as you folks were in bed."

"Where else, at two o'clock in the morning?"

Nettie flushed. Jim's smile was varnish over the rough timber of his dislike. Lightfoot was a huge turkey-buzzard of a man, belligerent and bungling. He had got rich merely by getting onto this range first. It took more cleverness, now, but one day the likes of Lightfoot would be made to prove up on some of the range they claimed.

Lightfoot had a lofty nose and an oval-shaped black chinbeard. He inspected Nettie with a savoring curiosity. "I'm Rube Lightfoot, Missus Croft. I expect you've heard of me."

"I have, Mr. Lightfoot. You're quite famous."

Lightfoot rubbed whiskey from his chin. "Some of your people were quite famous, too, ma'am. I hope none of your lodge was at Little Rosebud. I lost a brother there."

"Those were Sioux, Mr. Lightfoot. My mother's people were Cherokee. My father, you know, was a Scotch trader."

Jim shoved between them. "Boys, you aren't drinking." He refilled Lightfoot's cup and started around. Suddenly he heard Nettie cry out; he whirled, the jug lying across the crook of his arm. Dave Banta had picked her up by the waist and was holding her so that her dark brushed hair was against the herringbone rip-rapping of the ceiling. A tall, skinny man in overalls, Banta had eyebrows and mustaches as yellow as chick fuzz.

"Always heard you couldn't creep up on an Injun!" he said. "Dang lie!"

The men in the cabin, Jim thought, would gag on their laughter. They slapped their legs and hooted, and tall John Porter howled and slapped his palm against his mouth, making the gobbling cry they had heard from the darkness.

Jim stood with a grin pasted on his face, despising them.

Banta set the girl down. She smoothed her dress over her hips.

"Of course I'm only half Indian, or I'd heard you coming," she said. Then: "I could make coffee and biscuits."

"Never mind," said Lightfoot. "I only come over on business anyhow. Directly we'll go along."

"Business?" asked Jim. "With me?"

"Two things, Croft," Lightfoot said. "You're overworking that Tres Piedras pasture of mine. You figuring to set up a Cherokee village for those papooses you'll be getting soon? I moved your stuff off it today."

"My deed says it's mine. I'll move them back tomorrow."

Lightfoot smiled, and a hard light came into his eyes. "It ain't the place of a guest to contend with his host. We'll talk about it when you're guest under my roof, which will be next week. I'm going to barbecue some goats o' Saturday. You and your squaw can come if you like."

Banta chuckled, and for a moment Jim's jaw muscles marbled and he was on the point of stepping into the rancher. But then he said drily, "Sure, Rube. We'll be there."

Lightfoot signaled that the fun was over by opening the door and herding the others toward it and out into the yard.

You could hear them cackling clean to Sierra County, thought Jim, and he stood there and watched them trudge off to their horses. Back from the darkness came Dave Banta's shout.

"So long, Jim! Hold onto your scalp!"

He went back, ashamed before his wife. He had drunk with these men and fought with one or two; fought beside them during the Texas trail invasion. But by taking a half-breed wife, he had made himself a stranger to them.

Nettie's arms slipped around his neck. She smiled. "It's all right, Jim. They're just testing us."

"It will be all right," said Jim grimly, "if I have to horsewhip every man in Sacaton County!"

"What about the women? No, Jim," she said. "If I can't make them respect me for myself, your trouncing them won't help."

That was it, Jim realized. It was something he couldn't fight in the usual way. He snuffed the candle and punched a hole in the bolster with his head. "All right," he said. "I'll keep back. But if the big ox touches you, or his woman says any of the things they're askin' us over to say—I'll clean some plows right there."

"It wouldn't help, Jim. We could be proud and lonely, but I don't want to be lonely. I want friends, and friends for our children. I want them coming over to borrow things. I want neighbors, Jim, not next-door enemies."

Driving over Saturday morning, Jim kept tucking the blanket about her lap, making sure there wasn't space between them for a thickness of buckskin. It was March, with a few rags of snow under the junipers, brilliant against the red earth. The gray sky was slotted with bars of turquoise.

Nettie's coloring was earthy, her lips vivid, her eyes pale blue against dark lashes. Her being so pretty, he thought, would make it no easier for her to get on with the women.

Out under the oaks in Reuben Lightfoot's canyon-bottom home place, the smoke fumed deliciously in barbecue pits. A small army of neighbors had collected—thirty or forty ranchers, their wives and children. In the rough way of the country, the Lightfoot place was grand. The house was large, a low adobe structure without plaster; the corrals were rambling and tight; there was a barn with a sheet metal roof.

Rube was the grand and mannerless host, keeping the whiskey flowing while his guests waited for the goats to cook through. Dave Banta lugged a gallon lard can around, smearing tart comeback sauce on the carcasses. Lightfoot roared greetings to the Crofts and a couple of other families just arriving. Mrs. Lightfoot, a small woman with a florid skin and the figure of a sack of potatoes, collected the women.

"Come along and fresh up, ladies," she said. "You might as well come, too, Mrs. Croft."

Jim stopped dead. He looked at Nettie. It had gone into her like a knife. For an instant he thought she would cry. Then he heard her saying gravely, "I'd like to. Won't you call me Nettie?"

"If you want," said Mrs. Lightfoot coldly.

While she was gone, he toured around among these men he had not seen since his marriage. They all wanted to know where he had captured his squaw, and he told them the same thing, "Off a reservation; where else?"

"Well, look out for her, ever she goes on the warpath," said tall John Porter.

"Look out for any of them, when that happens," said Jim.

The women came back, and now the barbecue was ready, the savor of it tremendous in the air. Rube stuffed a dishtowel under his belt, whipped an edge onto a carving knife, and began to carve. Coffee bubbled endlessly from blackened kettles. Horseshoes clanged against a stake somewhere, and men leaned against trees and wagons, with pie tins balanced on their palms. But their eyes were never off Jim and his half-breed wife, and rebellion built steadily in him.

He heard Mrs. Lightfoot say to Nettie, "Tell us about your life at the trading post, girl."

It was suddenly quiet. They waited, like beggars, for the meanest slip they could twist into something laughable or damning.

"Why, it was nice, but lonesome. We'd be snowed in so long, and just the same faces all the time. I was awfully glad when—when I came down here. Everyone's been so friendly."

"Did you ever have trouble with—with savages?" asked Mrs. Lightfoot.

"Indians, you mean? No, not at our post. They were friendly."

"I expect it's all in knowing how to handle them."

"Yes."

"How do you handle them?" Mrs. Lightfoot asked, and you could hear nothing but a horseshoe clanging against an iron stake.

"Just as you'd like to be handled yourself," Nettie said softly.

Mrs. Lightfoot was stopped for a moment. Lucy Banta simpered, "What was your real name, Nettie? Laughing Water, or something?"

One of the younger women tittered. Jim slung his coffee grounds into the pit. The steam flared hotly. He saw Lucy Banta start as he went slowly toward her.

"She was born a Christian, Lucy. By the way, I heard they're taking bids for a herd of beef at the Territorial prison. You ought to get Dave to bid—combine business and pleasure, as you might say."

Mrs. Banta's brother was making hair bridles in Santa Fe,

having been caught with a small, select herd of whitefaces two years ago. Nettie arched an alarmed glance at Jim, but he would not back water. He stared Lucy Banta down.

Then he heard Rube Lightfoot's chuckle. "A cowthief," he said, "is just a nester that got caught. That's fine talk from you, Squawman."

Jim was seized with a cold and reckless fury. He turned quickly on Lightfoot, gripping the bosom of his buckskin shirt and ramming his back against a tree.

"That's one thing nobody calls me, Rube. Just nobody!"

The rancher grinned, his face larded with a bland satisfaction. "What do we call you—Gin'ral?"

"Anything except that." Jim was conscious that silence had invaded the yard. Everyone watched. Everyone listened.

Rube gathered his malice in his mouth like spittle. He said softly, "Settin' yourself a big task, Jim, if you aim to whip every man that looks crostwise at you. I figure you don't make a thing something it ain't by telling other folks it's so. If it's there, they'll see it."

"If what's there?"

"What you want them to see."

"I don't want them to see squawman on me, Rube. That's what I'm saying. And you'd better not be talking about anybody else in my family."

The moment was thick; it ended with Mrs. Lightfoot's crying, "Well, land, we ain't touched the pies yet!"

Lightfoot, with a wink at Dave Banta, went to the house. Jim's shoulders made a settling motion, like a dog laying the hairs on his back. He hitched up his belt and looked around. At once he saw that he had blundered. Nettie was biting her lip to keep from crying. He had done what she had begged him not to. He had demanded something that could not be taken by force—respect for his wife. He had, by challenging Rube, merely shamed her.

He put aside the rest of his food and went to watch a horseshoe game.

The sun began to drift deeper into the hills. For hours, no one had stopped eating. Most of the men, including Lightfoot, had not stopped drinking. A lot of ranch wives would do the driving on the way home. He had a desperate desire to do something to make amends; he had this desire and at the same time wanted to crush them all with some supreme blow.

As it neared leaving time, Jim became aware that the men were ribbing Lightfoot up to something. When he was drunk, he always did feats of strength. He had already hoisted a calf over his head and wrestled down half the men in sight. Now, with Banta grinning at his side, he swaggered over to Jim.

"Injun-rassle you two out of three, Gin'ral," he said.

Nettie was shaking her head. Mrs. Lightfoot and the other ladies watched with cockfight eagerness behind their proper faces.

Jim looked Rube over. "Figure you can make it interesting for me?"

"Bet a long yearlin' you won't be bored."

Jim hitched up his pants and lay on the ground. Loaded with food and liquor, Lightfoot arranged his arms and legs for the best purchase. The men swarmed around them as they raised their legs on signal and began sparring. Rattlesnake-quick, Jim's foot caught Lightfoot's ankle. A single heave threw the rancher out of position.

Jim laughed, while Rube swore and began claiming he had not been ready. Dave Banta laughed. "Ready as you'd ever be, Rube. Tally one for Jim."

Lightfoot's face was swollen with fury. He lay back. Banta called time and their legs went up. Cagey this time, Lightfoot feinted. Abruptly locking his knee about Jim's leg, he gave a sideward yank. Jim turned his leg and let the man's weight slough aside. With a surprised gasp, Rube rocked onto his side. He grunted, "Anybody can run!" and began to spar again.

Immediately Jim caught the fat leg with his heel and threw Lightfoot onto his face.

He sprang up. Banta and the others hooted at the rancher's protests. Lightfoot came up, looking sick and ugly.

"I hope all your kids are born with feathers in their hair, Croft," he said.

For a moment, Jim could almost feel his pulpy mouth on his knuckles. But after a moment his rage drained out of him. He was tired and defeated. He turned away, hating them all. He hated each one and he hated them as a clan. He despised them for the lonely years ahead of Nettie.

Remembering about the Tres Piedras pasture, he knew what he was going to say. He would tell Rube to keep the hell out, or there would be shooting trouble.

He was glad when the day finally ended. Darkness stifled the big ranchyard. Children began to fuss and livestock bawled in the pasture. Jim went to collect the pans in which Nettie had brought gooseberry pies. He found them in the kitchen, returning then to look for Nettie. But she had gone to the wagon in the trees.

As he entered the dark grove, Jim heard scuffling. He halted, listening. Nettie's voice came, low and taut. "Mr. Lightfoot! You aren't yourself."

The rancher's voice was choked with heat. "Don't be coy with old Rube, gal. I know Injun gals. Come on, now—"

Jim was striding through the dark. He heard Nettie sobbing with hurt and shame, "Mr. Lightfoot!"

Lightfoot was a hunched, bearish back. All Jim could see of Nettie was her face over his shoulder. Rube's mouth was pressed against the hollow of her throat. At the last instant he heard Jim. He swerved away and came slowly about.

Jim's fist collided with his cheekbone. It made a sharp, meaty slap.

Rube reeled back against a wagonshaft. Nettie cried out and came between them. The horse reared. Thrusting her aside, Jim met the rancher. Lightfoot's fist boomed against his chest. Jim hit him a savage chop on the ear. Lightfoot was driven to the ground, but he seized Jim's leg and pulled himself up.

A lantern was swinging in quick arcs through the trees. "What's all the rannikaboo, there, Rube?" someone shouted. Mrs. Lightfoot's cry came with a lacing of fear, "Reuben!"

Jim squared off, his fist cocked. Rube's face was a blank, bruised target. He looked scared. Jim savored the moment. Lightfoot had had his day of shaming others, and now he was about to be shamed before his wife and guests. He would never again ride into town without seeing hands raised to whispering mouths.

But it was suddenly Nettie's face before Jim, and her hands were against his chest. "No, Jim!" she said urgently. Jim thrust her away. "Jim, please! For me! You promised . . ."

When Dave Banta arrived to hold his lantern above the men and the girl and the rearing horse, Jim stood with his long arms hanging. Rube looked drunk and foolish. The tableau lingered until Mrs. Lightfoot and the rest crowded in. Jim saw the shame and terror on her face. He was oddly touched—troubled that she must suffer, too.

Abruptly Nettie turned toward Rube. She touched his bruised cheekbone, exclaiming in sympathy. "Oh, it's going to blacken, Rube! We're so sorry—Jim," she cried, "I asked you not to use that horse. Why, he's just a half-trained bronc!"

Jim was stopped. Nettie pulled Rube away from the shafts. Dave Banta seized a cheekstrap to drag the horse down.

"Look out for him," Nettie cautioned. "He's a terror to club you with his head. Why, Rube was just harnessing him for me and he hit him without blinking an eye. He hit Jim only last week. On—on the right ear, wasn't it, Jim?"

Nettie's eyes were begging him. " . . . The left," said Jim. "I wouldn't have taken him, only he was handy. Rube, I reckon I owe you an apology." His mouth barely smiled.

Rube stirred out of his paralysis. "Sho'. I ought to know a skittish horse when I see one. My fault, Jim."

His wife, thought Jim, had the eyes of a grateful dog. She was looking gently at Nettie. "Don't feel sorry for the man," she said. "Maybe the horse just knows a drunken old fool when it sees one."

Jim shouted his laughter, and that was the end of it. Rube took their banter, fussed with the harness, and finally the four of them were alone. Jim tucked the robe about Nettie, straight and dark-haired on the seat. As he put his foot up to mount, Mrs. Lightfoot spoke hesitantly.

"He—he does the most outlandish things when he's drinking, Nettie."

"Your husband's a great one to chivaree, that's all. He might have fooled me, only Jim told me beforehand, 'Rube's a great josher. But he's got a heart as good as gold'."

"Did Jim say that? Well, Rube's a diamond in the rough, only sometimes—"

Just as the wagon ground away, Rube called, "You go ahead and use that pasture, Jim. What's the use of good neighbors argifying over a little old buck-pasture like that'n?"

In the darkness, Nettie's eyes met Jim's, moist and laughing, and Jim knew it was over. They would come no more in the night, insinuating, and trying them. When they came, it would be as friends.

DANGEROUS ORDERS

Les Savage, Jr.

SOME of the most accomplished Western short stories of the period 1947–1954 were published in Zane Grey's Western Magazine. *Technically, ZGWM was not a pulp; it was a digest-size magazine. But in its aim, its contents, and even the paper on which it was printed, it was indeed a pulp (just as* Western Story *remained one for the last six years of its life, after Street & Smith shrank it to digest size early in 1944). Under the editorship of Don Ward, ZGWM published original fiction by most of the major names in the Western field, as well as classic reprints by Zane Grey and other pioneers and a variety of nonfiction pieces. Ward was especially good at developing new writers; among his "finds" was Elmore Leonard, who sold many of his early stories to Ward.*

Les Savage, Jr. (1922–1958) was already an established young professional when "Dangerous Orders," one of his and ZGWM's best stories, appeared in 1951. Savage began writing in the early forties, selling his first story to the first pulp he submitted it to, and soon abandoned an early desire to be an artist to write Western and historical fiction full time. His maiden novel, Treasure of the Brasada, *was published in 1947; he followed it with upwards of a dozen more, including such outstanding hardcover titles as* Shadow Riders of the Yellowstone *(1951) and* Hangtown *(1956), and several paperback originals under the pseudonym of Logan Stewart. He also wrote for episodic television in the fifties. The best of his fiction compares favorably with that of Luke Short, Wayne D, Overholser, and other of his major contemporaries. But Savage died tragically young, of a heart ailment at age 36, and his work has never received the recognition it deserves. Had he lived to continue his literary growth and development, he would unquestionably have become one of the traditional Western's brightest stars.*

Lieutenant John Hunter, First Dragoons, stood beside his two big cavalry mounts on Tucson's *Calle Real,* watching the last Federal troops march eastward down the ancient street. It was June seventeenth, 1861. The withdrawal of Union troops for service in the East had loosed the long-restrained vengeance of the Apache. Southern Arizona was being laid waste, and refugees were streaming into Tucson, the only white outpost left for hundreds of miles.

The creaking wheels and tramping feet of the incoming mob beat up the dust till it filled the air with a mealy haze and settled in whispering white layers on the young lieutenant's uniform and face. It was a long and thoughtful face, already turned gaunt by the rigors of this land, with crevices of perpetual watchfulness at the corners of the eyes.

He straightened a little as he saw Sheridan Wade elbowing through the press. They had told Hunter it might start anytime. But somehow he had not considered Wade.

The tanned, youthful smoothness of Wade's face was a painful cultivation against the insidious signs of whitening hair and thickening belly which even the impeccable cut of his bottle-green frock coat failed to hide. He saw Hunter as he struggled free of the mob, and a genial smile curled his mouth.

"Aren't you going with your company, John?"

Hunter kept his face blank. "I'm on orders to Santa Fe."

Surprise seemed to widen Wade's tawny eyes a little too much. "What a wonderful coincidence, John. I'm bound there myself. The last stage left yesterday and the bank closed before I could get my money out. I haven't been able to get hold of a horse."

His gaze turned covetous as it settled on Hunter's extra animal, and the lieutenant spoke sharply.

"That's my spare, Wade. I can't let anybody have it."

"What a way to treat an old friend," Wade said chidingly. He grasped Hunter's arm. "You have no idea how happy I was to find you stationed so close to Tucson when I came here last March, John. I swear I'd have seen more of you if I hadn't been so infernally busy. But now we've got to make up for it. You can't turn down a man from your own hometown, boy—"

"I'm sorry, Wade," Hunter said.

Wade's hand slid off; it seemed an effort to keep the paternal indulgence in his chuckle. "You must be doing something infernally important to be so damn stiff."

Something slyly knowing licked through Wade's eyes. "Is it this last order issued by department headquarters at Santa Fe, John? All commanders in the Territory were to destroy what supplies they couldn't transport when they evacuated, weren't they? It's common knowledge that Apache raids have kept Fort Warren cut off from Santa Fe for months. Warren probably got the first order—to evacuate—on the twentieth of June. It was sent out some time ago. But they couldn't possibly have gotten this new order to destroy, could they?"

Hunter could hardly keep the shock from his face. How could the man know so much? If Fort Warren didn't get the order to destroy what supplies they couldn't carry, they'd move out in three days, leaving behind them enough stores for a regiment. It was as if Wade had read Hunter's mind.

"The only way Fort Warren could get the order to destroy is for one of the commanders down here to relay it by messenger," the older man said. "Are you the messenger, John?"

Hunter shook his head stiffly. "You've got it wrong, Wade."

"In a way, I hope I have," Wade said. "You must know the

Confederates will have an agent out to stop those orders from reaching Fort Warren. You must know what that agent is capable of doing to attain his ends."

"You—Wade?" There was a soft disbelief in Hunter's voice.

The man chuckled heartily. "Lord Harry no, John. I'm just a banker. You know that. I only come to you as a friend."

He grasped Hunter's arm again. "Baylor and his Confederates are within a day's march of Tucson right now. They need supplies desperately. Those stores at Fort Warren would mean the difference between taking Arizona or not. All you'd have to do is see that the order to destroy doesn't reach Fort Warren, John. As simple as that. You can't let your own people down."

"You talkin' about white trash, Wade?" John asked softly.

Anger mottled the man's cheeks, but he checked it with palpable effort. "Don't be like that. It's in the past. We're both in this together now, John. We're both fighting for the South."

Hunter's eyes were narrowed to slits. "What South, Wade? Yours or mine? Do you think mine's worth fighting for? Do you think I'd have left if I'd wanted to fight for it? A one-room shanty on a stinking backwater and a rag for a shirt and a handful of hominy—"

Wade held up a protesting hand. "John—"

"Or your South, Wade? You wouldn't give me a crumb of it before. Mint juleps and white houses and dimity women. Would Lucy speak to me on the street now? Would you keep me standing all evenin' at the back door with my hat in my hand now—"

"Damn you, shut up!" Wade had leaned so close their faces almost touched. Though his voice was barely a whisper, it was as venomous as a snake's hiss. "I made the mistake of treating you like a gentleman. Now I'm goin' to treat you like the white trash you are. No wonder my daughter laughed at you when you asked to court her. Lucy knew what you were, even better'n I. And it didn't change you none to run away.

I'm through askin', John. I'm tellin'. I'm ridin' with you, and if you don't take me you know what will happen. There are a hundred Confederate sympathizers in this town that would jes' love to know you're carryin' those orders to Fort Warren."

Hunter felt his belly knot up with violent reaction. But somehow he checked himself, the blood pounding hotly through his head. Dimly, he realized Wade was right. A hundred sympathizers. They'd be on his tail the moment Wade told them. And it wasn't the sympathizers Hunter wanted. He stared at Wade, realizing what he would have to do. He felt his shoulders sag in defeat.

"All right, Wade," he said in a low voice. "Let's go."

He saw triumphant justification lick through Wade's tawny eyes. A justification of Wade's whole class, his whole way of life. The man settled back with a smug smile, squaring his coat with a pull at the lapels.

"Yes," he said, with a return of that lubricious geniality. "By all means, let's go."

The road unfurled like a saffron banner before the two men as they trotted northward from Tucson. The sun cast grotesque shadows at the foot of mesas flung like giant blockhouses across the desert. A field of sacaton grass slipped over the horizon, turned to a glittering sea by the brazen sun.

Hunter rode hunched forward in the saddle, eyes tirelessly moving across the endless expanse of earth which swept at last into the Superstitions lying in a jagged silhouette against the sky.

The lieutenant's mind was on Wade, at his side. He could not see the man's face, but he knew the expression it held: It seemed to symbolize the insidious pressures which had driven Hunter from his home in the first place. He had tried since early boyhood to rise above the degraded level at which his birth as the son of a river rat had placed him. He had battered his head for years against the cottony wall of patronization and tacit exclusion by Wade's decaying society. Perhaps the final blow had been Wade's daughter.

Hunter had worshipped Lucy Wade from childhood. As long as he had kept it impersonal, she had tolerated him. He had even taken a job as a stable boy on the Wade plantation—when few white men would be seen at such a task—to be near her. He could ride behind her on the hunt and drive her gig to town when she shopped. There had been a certain comradeship between them even under those circumstances. He had been blind to the patronization. But finally he had been unable to contain himself. He had told her how he felt.

Hunter could still hear her laughter, rich with derision and contempt. The whole town had known the next day. The whole town had laughed.

He had run from her laughter. Also he had run from something deeper. More than anything else, it had made him realize the futility of trying to change his station in such a society.

Wade's voice broke in on Hunter's thoughts. "Can't I have another drink, John? My throat's closing up."

Their canteens made a hollow clanking against the flanks of Hunter's horse, as he turned to look at Wade. The desert was beginning to take its toll. Wade lagged behind Hunter, his soft weight settled deeply into the saddle. But that smug haughtiness still lay in his eyes.

Hunter knew what was going through the man's mind. Wade thought the lieutenant would comply with this as he would have back in Virginia, bowing automatically to hereditary authority, reverting without a struggle to the old servility. That was the worst for Hunter. Knowing he could not strike back. Knowing he could not show the man how different the standards were out here; how a man's worth didn't depend upon his birth or his wealth; how he, himself, had changed.

"We drink at four, Wade," he said. "We don't reach water

till night. I don't see how you ever thought you'd get through alone."

"I'd have managed," Wade said condescendingly. "My home office in Richmond needed a man to get what Confederate funds he could out of Santa Fe, before the Union confiscated them."

He broke off to cough as a hot wind swept parched dust into their faces. Then he brought his horse against Hunter, reaching for the canteen. "Damn it, John, give me a drink."

Hunter reined his horse sharply away.

"Don't crowd me, Wade," he said. "We drink at four."

Wade's eyes widened in surprise. Then the expression changed within them, and his mouth furled with contempt.

"White trash is gettin' high and mighty ideas again," he said.

Hunter's voice came out thinly. "You haven't got your hundred Confederate sympathizers out here, Wade."

The man settled back into his saddle, studying Hunter with a new calculation in his eyes. But he spoke derisively. "Think I'd really need them, John?"

Hunter glanced at him, trying to read all the implications in his face. Then he gigged his horse on ahead.

The heat seemed to grow greater through the afternoon. Hunter was seeing mirages now, lakes in the middle of a dry salt flat, cities where only the gnarled saguaro grew. They came to eroded bluffs and dismounted for a rest in the meager shade. Hunter was barely on his feet before he saw the prints in the sand.

"Get aboard, Wade."

The man had just lowered himself against the sandy *barranca*, and looked up in surprise. "What for? We've got to rest."

"Not here. Can't you see those hoofprints? It's an Indian war party and it passed here within the hour."

To the east were badlands, gullies, and fissures cut by centuries of wind and water into a weird labyrinth without end. They sought cover here and sweated without shade for the rest of the afternoon.

Hunter lay on his belly against a bank, scanning the sky in all directions with his four-power cavalry binoculars. At last he saw the stain against the ruddy banners of evening clouds. He let Wade see it.

"Smoke," he said. "It would come up in puffs if they were signaling. They've burned out somebody. We'll head toward it."

An edge of tension ripped at the cultivated geniality of Wade's voice. "Why go directly toward them?"

"Because they're about finished when they start a fire. They won't backtrack. They're out looking for something else to raid now and they didn't find anything on their way through here."

Night darkened the sky till the smoke was no longer visible as a separate hue. They halted a few minutes for a cold supper from the lieutenant's saddlebags. The moon had risen by the time they reached the gutted buildings. Smoke still curled dismally into the night, and somewhere off a wolf was howling.

"This is our first water hole," Hunter said. "It's the Chicataw way station."

Seeing no sign of bodies within, Hunter led around the buildings to the rocky sink. He dropped his reins to the ground and hunkered down, scooping up a handful of water. He tasted it and spat it out.

"They've dumped alkali into the water," he said. "We can't use it."

Wade's rigging squawked as he swung off, his mouth starting to open in horrified protest. Before he could speak, there was a sharp rattle from the brush across the sink. Wade's hand darted instinctively inside his frock coat.

Moonlight spilled across the figure of the man who crawled feebly from the sagebrush across the water.

"I thought you was them warwhoops at first," he said feebly.

Hunter rose from his squatting position, hand still on the butt of his holstered Dragoon Colt, giving a glance to the snub-nosed derringer Wade had pulled from under his coat.

"I didn't know you carried a gun, Wade," he said.

There was a flutter of guilt in Wade's eyes. He shoved the derringer back into its harness under his lapel. His chuckle held a forced urbanity.

"Ace in the hole, John, ace in the hole."

Hunter was already hooking a canteen from his horse and moving around the tip of the sink. The third man sat heavily back into the sand, reaching eager hands up to hold the canteen as Hunter tipped it to his lips. He was a big raw-boned figure with long-sleeved red woolens for his shirt and a pair of grease-blackened rawhide leggins stuffed into cast-off cavalry boots.

"You're Hock Ellis, aren't you?" Hunter asked.

"That's right, Lieutenant. Station-keeper here. I was the only one left when them warwhoops jumped the station. I got out the back way and hid in the bushes. Been there without water all day. Damn sun clabbered my brains."

Hunter frowned suspiciously at him. "I thought that last stage out of Tucson was going to pick up all personnel as far as Salt River."

Ellis got unsteadily to his feet, handing the canteen back. "That's what saved me, I guess. Them Apaches thought the crew here had left and didn't bother hunting for me."

"We can't take you," Wade said. "We'll be lucky if we make it ourselves to the next water hole."

A wild look widened Ellis's eyes, then he caught at the pommel of Wade's horse. "You got to take me along with you, them Apaches are everywhere—"

Wade caught Ellis by one arm and jerked him loose, spinning him back so hard the man tripped and fell. Ellis rolled over onto his belly, staring dazedly at Wade.

"I wouldn't have thought you were that strong," Hunter told Wade.

The man turned sharply, almost angrily. Then he collected his gentility with effort, and that oily chuckle slipped from him.

"You don't want to underestimate us bankers, John."

Hunter's eyes traveled back to the station-keeper, seeking some capacity for guile, for intrigue, in the man's equine face. He could read nothing but grim weariness. Then the irony of this struck him and he could not help a grim smile.

"Ellis will ride with you," Hunter told Wade.

Wade stared blankly, "We'll never make it. Three men on two horses. No water. All those Apaches between us and the Salt River. You're crazy, John—"

"But still a white man, Wade. Let Ellis get on first."

A raw wind mourned down off the Superstitions. It rattled through miles of creosote brush like the beat of an Indian tom-tom. It made Hunter shiver and huddle in his tunic.

The stage station was hours behind. Sheridan Wade's horse was beginning to falter beneath the double load. They had given the last of their water to the animals. Hunter knew if they didn't come up with the next sink before dawn they would have to spend all day without water. It was too risky to travel during the day with Apaches all around.

He began to keep his eyes open for a safe campsite. He was so intent on this that he did not notice how Wade's horse was lagging behind. Suddenly he realized it was no longer visible from the tail of his eye, and he jerked sharply around in the saddle. The two men were a full length back of him, Wade sitting behind Ellis.

"What's the matter, Lieutenant?" Ellis said. "You look like the cat caught stealing the cream."

"Get ahead of me where I can see you," Hunter said.

The station-keeper gigged the horse up. "What makes you so suspicious? You ain't got any more water left to steal."

"Perhaps he's wondering what your politics are," Wade said.

"I'm the best Unionist of 'em all," Ellis said. Then he spat disgustedly. "How do you get off wondering about my politics, Lieutenant, you traveling with a damn Secesh banker from Virginia?"

"Don't rile the lieutenant," Wade said smugly. "He'd like to forget his origins."

Ellis glanced at Hunter's hands. The calluses were beginning to wear off, but the gaunt knobbiness that came from a lifetime of common labor would never leave. The station-keeper read the story.

"You didn't git to live up in the big house, I guess, sipping them juleps and watching them pretty horses." His voice grew sly. "Is that what they call white trash down there, Lieutenant?"

Hunter felt his ears begin to glow. Wade chuckled, and it was filled with husky mockery. Hunter's hands closed tight on the pommel, and he would not look at them.

"How did a man like you git to be an officer?" Ellis said. "You sure ain't West Point."

"He was always a good bootlicker," Wade murmured.

Hunter looked straight ahead. He could feel the blood beating at his temples. But he realized there was even more reason to contain himself now. He had seen it as ironic, at first, that they were forced to take Ellis with them. Now he realized it might contain more irony than he had bargained for.

"You never did tell us how you happened to get left at the station," he told Ellis thinly.

"No room on the coach. They left me a horse. But he got away."

"*Did* he now? Hunter said.

He saw surprise turn the man's seamed face blank. He jerked his head for them to go on. Ellis dug heels into his horse. Wade said something softly into the station-keeper's ear. Ellis laughed gutterally.

They found the rotting building in the darkest hours

before dawn. It was up in the wind-swept mesa land, crouched in the lee of a lonely bluff. Hunter checked his weary horse, peering through the thick texture of darkness at the ancient logs stacked into a beehive shape.

"We'll be safe," he said. "It's a *tchindi hogan*."

Wade frowned at him. "A what?"

"A devil house. See that hole in the north end? Some Navajo died here a long time ago. They knocked logs from the north wall and took him out there."

"Boy's right," Ellis said. "No warwhoop will ever go near this place again. Afraid the devils will get them."

Hunter tethered his horse and unsaddled. He stripped some kindling from the rotting logs that had been knocked out of the north wall, stooped in the low door with these.

He found the circle of rocks in the center where the ashes of countless fires lay in powdery dust, and stacked his kindling here. Then he ignited it. Flames licked upward, turning the film of alkali on his face to a mealy shimmer. Then his eyes widened with the complete surprise of it.

The light revealed an enormously fat man sitting in the far corner like some gross Buddha, holding a four barreled pepperbox in one hand. He had a flat-topped hat jammed so tight it left a ridge of flesh just beneath the band. There were greasy channels in the deep furrows of his face where the sweat had run down to drip off his pink chin and make dark stains on his marseille waistcoat.

"George Mott, gentlemen. At you service."

Ellis let out a low whistle. "Had me spooked, Mott."

Mott shrugged. "Apaches burned out Tubac. I thought it would be safer out of the Territory."

"We didn't see any sign in front," Hunter said.

"I hid my horse in a gully at the rear," Mott offered. He smiled slyly at Wade. "The banker from Virginia, I believe."

Hunter saw the little pucker of muscle run through Wade's face. The lieutenant remembered Mott now, an agent for some Santa Fe mining interests down around Tubac. The man had been through Tucson several times. His little eyes almost disappeared in their pouches of fat as they licked back across the room to Hunter.

"I understood most of the officers in the Territory were resigning their commissions in favor of the Confederacy."

"Is that what you understood?" Hunter said.

"He was traveling with Wade," Hock Ellis said.

"Well." Mott's chuckle shook his great belly. "Perhaps you and I are the only Black Republicans in the house, Hock."

Ellis snorted assent, easing himself to a sitting position against the wall, pulling his holstered cap and ball around so it lay between his legs.

"We'll have to draw a Mason-Dixon line right through the middle of this room," he said.

The heat of the fire was reaching Hunter, and he unbuttoned his tunic. "As I remember, there was a sink behind this hogan."

"Sink's still there," Mott said. "No water left."

Hunter saw the desperation momentarily swallow the antipathy lying between the men. Wade lowered himself to a seated position, taking out a handkerchief and dismally wiping the grime from around his mouth. Mott looked at the pepperbox in his hand, put the gun away. As Hunter sat down, the jackknifing of his body shoved the manila envelope up out of its inside pocket till a corner peaked from beneath the lapel of his tunic. He saw three pairs of eyes swing to it.

"Orders, Lieutenant?" Mott asked.

"To Santa Fe," Wade said sardonically.

"My, my," Mott said. "I've heard an order was also sent for Fort Warren to destroy all the supplies they couldn't transport."

"Wonder what'd happen if them orders didn't reach Fort Warren?" Ellis said, turning wonderfully innocent eyes on Hunter.

"They'd leave without destroying the supplies." Mott's grin

was cherubic. "The supplies would fall into the hands of the Confederates. It would practically give them Arizona."

"Them Johnny Rebs know about everything that's going on," Ellis said, "They must have an agent out to stop those orders."

"Or two agents," Mott said slyly, glancing at Wade.

"Or three?" asked Hunter, mildly.

Mott stared at him for a moment. Then a chuckle began to spread from the subterranean depths of him till the dank hogan was filled with great spasms of sound. Finally it settled back into the man and the hogan was quiet.

Despite Hunter's burning thirst, exhaustion bore heavily on him. He felt his eyelids drooping. The desire for sleep became overpowering. He drew on all his will to remain awake. He sensed the culmination of the whole thing coming.

Mott began snoring softly, fat chin sunk against his chest. Wade let out his breath and leaned back against the wall, closing his eyes. Again that urge to sleep hit Hunter. He heard Ellis stir, and felt his eyes snap open. But the station-keeper was only settling against the earth.

The fire seemed to fade out. Darkness gathered. Something cottony was closing in against Hunter. It was pain to fight it. Then something brought him awake again with that sick shock.

George Mott was staring across the fire at him with eyes sly as a weasel's.

Hunter shook his head, trying to clear it. At the same time there was a sharp whinny from outside, and the drum of excited hoofs. It brought Hunter instinctively to his feet, scattering the fire with a kick of his foot as he wheeled toward the door. He heard someone give a sharp cry as the coals hit and burned. Then he was plunging through the door with gun in hand.

He saw that it was his horse, running down off the slope with snapped reins. And even as he watched, the ungainly jackrabbit that had spooked the animal hopped off into the night.

Hunter went down the slope at a run. He knew the horse was too jaded to run far. He saw it slowing up ahead of him, and slowed himself so as not to frighten the animal further. He reached it and caught the reins and began to soothe it. He was several hundred yards from the house. The stars were out and the night was dead-black about him. Then he heard the first soft sound from behind him.

Quickly he tied the broken reins and led the horse a few paces to a creosote bush, hitching it firmly here. Then he walked directly away from it, making enough noise so they could hear him. Whatever happened he didn't want the horse to be spooked again. And he knew about what was going to happen.

He reached a gully filled with the acrid taint of greasewood. He moved down this for a dozen yards till he came to a dead end. He started to crawl up out of it when he heard the sound again. It was nearer. Already the pitch-blackness just before dawn was beginning to dissipate. He knew how swiftly light would come now. He had another moment to act.

If he left the gully now he would be trapped out on the flats without cover when light hit. Yet he would be just as effectively trapped in this dead end if he remained. There was the faintest crackle of greasewood before a moving body. Then silence again.

He took off his cap and tunic. He bellied up against the bank till he reached a greasewood bush on the east lip of the gully. Pearly streaks began to drift through the blackness of the sky. He found an outthrust branch upon which to slide the arm of his tunic, wrapping the body of it around and pulling in the other branches till he could button it. Then he put his forage cap on the top branch. He slid back into the gully.

The pearly streaks were spreading out until there was no blackness left. He began to crawl up the other side of the gully. In another moment it would be light. There was more noise from the other end. He reached the western lip of the gulch. On the other lip across from him, the first of full dawn silhouetted the tunic, arm outstretched toward the sun. He grabbed up a handful of rocks and threw them across the gulch. They landed by the silhouette with a sharp crackling.

There was another vicious crackling of brush from the bottom of the gully, twenty feet down from the end, and the sudden blast of a gun. He saw the silhouetted tunic jerk. His Navy revolver bucked in his hand as he fired at the other gun flashes. He squeezed the trigger three times and then stopped. The echoes ran out into the desert and grew flat and small and died. The stench of black powder lay heavy on the air.

Finally Hunter edged on his belly through the bushes along the edge of the gulch till he came over the place where the fat man sat slumped in the sandy bottom. The front of him was soaked with blood, and his pepperbox had dropped in the sand.

"You're the only one?" Hunter said.

Mott's chin sank onto his chest. "That's right, son. I saw you in Tucson when all the other troops had gone. I figured you were the messenger. I got out ahead of you. The Indian sign drove me here. I figured it would drive you here too. There was hardly another route you could take. You'd know the safety in a *tchindi hogan*. So I waited—"

The last left him on a sigh, and his eyes closed. In a moment, Sheridan Wade moved around a turn in the gulch, staring at the dead man.

"I thought you were the one, Wade," Hunter said.

Wade was staring dully at Mott, his shoulders sagging, his voice strangely dull.

"Just a banker, John," he said wearily. "I told you that. I guess I had some idea of trying for the orders, if the agent didn't show up. I guess it doesn't matter now, does it?"

There was a rattling of greasewood behind Hunter, and

Hock Ellis rose up, his cap-and-ball pointed at the lieutenant. "Maybe you'd better let a real Unionist take them orders the rest of the way."

Hunter turned, then silently pulled them from his pocket. Ellis opened the manila sheaf. Then his mouth parted in surprise.

"This is blank paper."

"The real orders are on their way by another route," Hunter said. "We knew the Confederates would probably have an agent out to stop them. I was supposed to decoy that agent."

He was watching Wade as he said it. The man stared at Hunter as if trying to understand something almost beyond his comprehension. His voice sounded weak.

"Then all the time—you only made me think—"

"Yes, Wade," Hunter said. "I had to let you believe nothing had changed. That you were still quality, and I was trash. I had to find out if you were the agent."

He saw the final understanding turn Wade to a defeated little old man. He tried to feel triumph. But Lucy and the past were too far away. He drew a heavy breath, turned to see Hock Ellis holding the papers out to him.

"I guess the things that make for quality or trash out here are a little different than they were back in Virginia," he said. "You've proved that to me as well as him, son. If these were the real orders, you'd be the man to take them. I owe you an apology. I'm only the second-best Unionist in the country. Kin I shake hands with the first?"

LAW OF THE HUNTED ONES

Elmore Leonard

ONE of the most intense and successful Western films is based on a pulp story: 3:10 to Yuma, *starring Glenn Ford and Van Heflin, from Elmore Leonard's short of the same title (*Dime Western, 1953*). Another Leonard pulp story, "The Captives," originally published in* Argosy *in 1955, was the basis for the excellent Randolph Scott film,* The Tall T. *The cinematic quality of his writing is just as evident in the dozens of other well-crafted tales of Old Arizona he contributed to the Western and adventure pulps in the late forties and early fifties—tales such as "Law of the Hunted Ones," taken from the December 1952 issue of* Western Story *(a short-lived Popular Publications revival of the Street & Smith title which had ceased publication in 1949), and never before reprinted.*

*Two of Leonard's Western novels also made significant films—*Hombre, *with Paul Newman, from the 1961 book considered by many to be among the best Westerns of all time; and* Valdez is Coming, *featuring Burt Lancaster, also from the novel of the same title (1970). Outstanding among his other full-length Westerns are* The Bounty Hunters *(1953),* Escape from Five Shadows *(1956), and* Forty Lashes Less One *(1972). In the past few years Leonard has achieved bestseller status with such tough crime novels as* Glitz *(1985), but his achievements in the field of popular Western literature remain the most accomplished and memorable of all his work.*

Patman saw it first. The sudden flash of sun on metal; then, on the steepness of the hillside, it was a splinter of a gleam that hung unmoving amidst the confusion of jagged rock and brush. Just a dull gleam now that meant nothing, but the first metallic flash had been enough for Virgil Patman.

He exhaled slowly, dropping his eyes from the gleam up on the slanting wall, and let his gaze drift up ahead through the narrowness, the way it would naturally. But his fists remained tight around the reins. He muttered to himself, "You damn fool." Cover was behind, a hundred feet or more, and a rifle can do a lot of pecking in a hundred feet.

The boy doesn't see it, he thought. Else he would have been shooting by now. And then other words followed in his mind. Why do you think the boy's any dumber than you are?

He shifted his hip in the saddle and turned his head halfway around. Dave Fallis was a few paces behind him and to the side. He was looking at his hands on the flat dinner-plate saddle horn, deep in thought.

Patman drew tobacco and paper from his side coat pocket and held his mount in until the boy came abreast of him.

"Don't look up too quick and don't make a sudden move," Patman said. He passed the paper along the tip of his tongue, then shaped it expertly in his bony, freckly fingers. He wasn't looking at the boy, but he could sense his head come up fast. "What did I just tell you!"

He struck a match and held it to the brown paper ciga-rette. His eyes were on the match and he half mumbled with the cigarette in his mouth. "Dave, hold on to your nerve. There's a rifle pointing at us. Maybe two hundred feet ahead and almost to the top of the slope." He handed the makings across. "Build yourself one like it was Sunday afternoon on the front porch."

Their horses moved at a slow walk close to the left side that was smooth rock and almost straight up. Here, and as far as you could see ahead, the right side slanted steeply up, gravel, rock, and brush thrown violently together, to finally climb into dense pines overhead. Here and there the pines strag-gled down the slope. Patman watched the boy put the twisted cigarette between his lips and light it, the hand steady, up close to his face.

"When you get a chance," Patman said, "look about halfway up the slope, just this side of that hollow. You'll see a dab of yellow that's prickly pear, then go above to that rock jam and tell me what you see."

Fallis pulled his hat closer to his eyes and looked up-canyon before dragging his gaze to the slope. His face registered nothing, not even a squint with the hat brim resting on his eyebrows. A hard-boned face, tight through the cheeks and red-brown from the sun, but young and with a good mouth that looked as if it smiled most of the time, though it wasn't smiling now. His gaze lowered to the pass and he drew on the cigarette.

"Something shining up there, but I don't make out what it is," he said.

"It's a rifle, all right. We'll take for granted somebody's behind it."

"Indian?"

"Not if the piece is so clean it shines," Patman answered. "Just keep going, and watch me. We'll gamble that it's a white man—and gamble that he acts like one."

Fallis tried to keep his voice even. "What if he just shoots?" The question was hoarse with excitement. Maybe the boy's not as scared as I am, Patman thought. Young and too eager to be afraid. You get old and take too damn much time doing what kept you alive when you were young. Why keep thinking of him, he thought, you got a hide too, you know.

Patman answered, "If he shoots, we'll know where we stand and you can do the first thing that comes to your mind."

"Then I might let go at you," Fallis smiled, "for leading us into this jackpot."

Patman's narrow face looked stone-hard with its sad smile beneath the full mustache. "If you want to make jokes," he said, "go find someone else."

"What're we going to do, Virg?" Fallis was dead serious. It made his face look tough when he didn't smile, with the heavy cheekbones and the hard jawline beneath.

"We don't have a hell of a lot of choices," Patman said. "If we kick into a run or turn too fast, we're likely to get a bullet. You don't want to take a chance on that gent up there being the nervous type. And if we just start shooting, we haven't got anyhting to hide behind when he shoots back."

He heard the boy say, "We can get behind our horses."

He answered him, "I'd just as soon get shot as have to walk home. You got any objections to just going on like we don't know he's there?"

Fallis shook his head, swallowing. "Anything you say, Virg. Probably he's just out hunting turkeys. . . . " He dropped behind the older man as they edged along the smooth rock of the canyon wall until there was ten feet between their horses.

They rode stiff-backed, from habit, yet with an easy looseness of head and arms that described an absence of tension. Part of it was natural, again habit, and part was each trying to convince the other that he wasn't afraid. Patman and Fallis were good for each other. They had learned it through campaigning.

Now, with the tightness in their bellies, they waited for the sound. The clop of their horses' hooves had a dull ring in the awful silence. They waited for another sound.

Both men were half expecting the heavy report of a rifle. They steeled themselves against the worst that could happen, because anything else would take care of itself. The sound of the loose rock glancing down the slope was startling, like a warning to jerk their heads to the side and up the slanting wall.

The man was standing in the spot where Patman had pointed, his rifle at aim, so that all they could see was the rifle below the hat. No face.

"Don't move a finger, or you're dead!" The voice was full and clear. The man lowered the rifle and called, "Sit still while I come down."

He turned and picked his way over the scattered rock, finally half sliding into the hollow that was behind his position. The hollow fell less steeply to the canyon floor with natural rock footholds and gnarled brush stumps to hold on to.

For a moment the man's head disappeared from view, then was there again just as suddenly. He hesitated, watching the two men below him and fifty feet back up the trail. Then he disappeared again into a deeper section of the descent.

Dave Fallis's hand darted to the holster at his hip.

"Hold onto yourself!" Patman's whisper was a growl in his heavy mustache. His eyes flicked to the hollow. "He's not alone! You think he'd go out of sight if he was by himself!"

The boy's hand slid back to the saddle horn while his eyes traveled over the heights above him. Only the hot breeze moved the brush clumps.

The man moved toward them on the trail ahead with short, bowlegged steps, his face lowered close to the upraised rifle. When he was a dozen steps from Patman's horse, his head came up and he shouted, "All right!" to the heights behind them. Fallis heard Patman mumble, "I'll be damned," looking at the man with the rifle.

"Hey, Rondo!" Patman was grinning his sad smile down at the short, bowlegged man with the rifle. "What you got here, a toll you collect from anybody who goes by?" Patman laughed out, with a ring of relief to the laugh. "I saw you a ways back. Your toll box was shining in the sun." He went on laughing and put his hand in his side coat pocket.

The rifle came up full on his chest. "Keep your hand in sight!" The man's voice cut sharply.

Patman looked at him surprised. "What's the matter with you, Rondo? It's me. Virg Patman." His arm swung to his side. "This here's Dave Fallis. We rode together in the Third for the past five years."

Rondo's heavy-whiskered face stared back, the deep lines unmoving as if they had been cut into stone. The rifle was steady on Patman's chest.

"What the hell's the matter with you!" Patman repeated. "Remember me bringing you your bait for sixty days at Thomas?"

Rondo's beard separated when his mouth opened slightly. "You were on the outside, if I remember correctly."

Patman swore with a gruff howl. "You talk like I passed sentence! You damn fool, what do you think a Corporal of the Guard is—a judge?" His head turned to Fallis. "This bent-legged waddie shoots a reservation Indian, gets sixty days, then blames it on me. You remember him in the lock-up?"

"No. I guess—"

"That's right," Patman cut in. "That was before your time."

Rondo looked past the two men.

"That wasn't before my time." The voice came from behind the two men.

He was squatting on a hump that jutted out from the slope, just above their heads and a dozen or so feet behind them, and he looked as if he'd been sitting there all the time. When he looked at him, Fallis thought of a scavenger bird perched on the bloated roundness of a carcass.

It was his head and the thinness of his frame that gave that impression. His dark hair was cropped close to his skull, brushed forward low on his forehead and coming to a slight point above his eyebrows. The thin hair pointed down, as did the ends of a shadowy mustache that was just starting to grow, lengthening the line of his face, a face that was sallow-complexioned and squinting against the brightness of the afternoon.

He jumped easily from the hump, his arms outstretched and a pistol in each hand, though he wore only one holster on his hip.

Fallis watched him open-mouthed. He wore a faded

undershirt and pants tucked into knee-high boots. A string of red cotton was knotted tight to his throat above the opening of the undershirt. And with it all, the yellowish death's-head of a face. Fallis watched because he couldn't take his eyes from the man. There was a compelling arrogance about his movements and the way he held his head that made Fallis stare at him. And even with the shabbiness of his dress, it stood out. It was there in the way he held his pistols. Fallis pictured a saber-slashing captain of cavalry. Then he saw a black-bearded buccaneer.

"I remember when Rondo was in the lock-up at Fort Thomas." His voice was crisp, but low and he extra-spaced his words. "That was a good spell before you rode me to Yuma, wasn't it?"

Patman shook his head. The surprise had already left his face. He shook his head wearily as if it was all way above him. He said, "If you got any more men up there that I policed, get 'em down and let me hear it all at once." He shook his head again. "This is a real day of surprises. I can't say I ever expected to see you again, De Sana."

"Then what are you doing here?" The voice was cold-clear, but fell off at the end of the question as if he had already made up his mind why they were there.

Patman saw it right away.

It took Fallis a little longer because he had to fill in, but he understood now, looking at De Sana and then to Patman.

Patman's voice was a note higher. "You think we're looking for you?"

"I said," De Sana repeated, "then what are you doing here?"

"Hell, we're not tracking you! We were mustered out last week. We're pointing toward West Texas for a range job, or else sign for contract buffalo hunters."

De Sana stared, but didn't speak. His hands, with the revolving pistols, hung at his sides.

"What do I care if you broke out of the Territory prison?"

Patman shouted it, then seemed to relax, to calm himself. "Listen," he said, "we're both mustered out. Dave here has got one hitch in, and I've got more years behind me than I like to remember. But we're out now and what the army does is its own damn business. And what you do is your business. I can forget you like that." He snapped his fingers. " 'Cause you don't mean a thing to me. And that dust-eatin' train ride from Wilcox to Yuma, I can forget that too, 'cause I didn't enjoy it any more than you did even if you thought then you weren't going to make the return trip. You're as bad as Rondo here. You think 'cause I was train guard it was my fault you got sent to Yuma. Listen, I treated you square. There were some troopers would have kicked your face in just on principle."

De Sana moistened his lower lip with his tongue, idly, thinking about the past and the future at the same time. A man has to believe in something, no matter what he is. He looked at the two men on the horses and felt the weight of the pistols in his hands. There was the easy way. He looked at them watching him uneasily, waiting for him to make a move.

"Going after a range job, huh?" he said almost inaudibly.

"That's right. Or else hunt buffalo. They say the railroad's paying top rate, too," Patman added.

"How do I know," De Sana said slowly, "you won't get to the next sheriff's office and start yelling wolf."

Patman was silent as his fingers moved over his jaw. "I guess you'll have to take my word that I've got a bad memory," he said finally.

"What kind of memory has your friend got?" De Sana said, looking hard at Dave Fallis.

"You got the biggest pistols he ever saw," Patman answered.

Rondo mounted behind Patman and pointed the way up the narrow draw that climbed from the main trail about a quarter of a mile up. It branched from the pass, twisting as it climbed, but more decidedly bearing an angle back in the direction from which they had come. Rondo had laughed out at Patman's last words. The tension was off now. Since De Sana had accepted the two men, Rondo would too, and went even a step further, talking about hospitality and coffee and words like "this calls for a celebration," even though the words were lost on the other three men. The words had no meaning but they filled in and lessened the tension.

De Sana was still standing in the pass when they left, but when Fallis looked back he saw the outlaw making his way up the hollow.

When the draw reached the end of its climb they were at the top of the ridge, looking down directly to the place where they had held up. Here, the pines were thick, but farther off they scattered and thinned again as they began to stretch toward higher, rockier ground.

De Sana was standing among the trees waiting for them. He turned before they reached him and led the way through the pines. Fallis looked around curiously, feeling the uneasiness that had come over him since meeting De Sana. Then, as he looked ahead, the hut wasn't fifty feet away.

It was a low structure, flat-roofed and windowless, with rough, uneven logs chinked in with adobe mud. On one side was a lean-to where the cooking was done. A girl was hanging strips of meat from the low ceiling when they came out of the pines, and as they approached she turned with a hand on her hip, smoothing a stray wisp of hair with the other.

She watched them with open curiosity, as a small child stares at the mystery of a strange person. There was a delicateness of face and body that accentuated this, that made her look nore childlike in her open sensitivity. De Sana glanced at her and she dropped her eyes and turned back to the jerked meat.

"Put the coffee on," De Sana called to her. She nodded her

head without turning around. "Rondo, you take care of the mounts and get back to your nest."

Rondo opened his mouth to say something but thought better of it and tried to make his face look natural when he took the reins from the two men and led the horses across the small clearing to the corral, part of which could be seen through the pines a little way off. A three-sided lean-to squatted at one end of the small, fenced area.

"That's Rondo's," De Sana pointed to the shelter. Walking to the cabin he called to the girl again. This time she did not shake her head. Fallis thought perhaps the shoulders tensed in the faded gray dress. Still, she didn't turn around or even answer him.

The inside of the cabin was the same as the outside, rough log chinked with adobe, and a packed dirt floor. A table and two chairs, striped with cracks and gray with age, stood in the middle of the small room. In a far corner was a straw mattress. On it, a blanket was twisted in a heap. Along the opposite wall was a section of log with a board nailed to it to serve as a bench, and next to this was the cupboard: three boxes stacked one on the other. It contained a tangle of clothing, cartridge boxes and five or six bottles of whiskey.

The two men watched De Sana shove his extra pistol into a holster that hung next to the cupboard. The other was on his hip. He took a half-filled bottle from the shelf and went to the table.

"Looks like I'm just in time." Rondo was standing in the doorway, grinning, with a canteen hanging from his hand. "Give me a little fill, *jefe*, to ease sitting on that eagle's nest."

De Sana's head came up and he moved around the table threateningly, his eyes pinned on the man in the doorway. "Get back to the pass!" His hand dropped to the pistol on his hip in a natural movement. "You watch! You get paid to watch! And if you miss anything going through that pass . . ." His voice trailed off, but for a moment it shook with excitement.

"Hell, Lew. Nobody's going to find us way up here," Rondo argued half-heartedly.

Patman looked at him surprised. "Cima Quaine's blood-dogs could track a man all the way to China."

"Aw, San Carlos's a hundred miles away. Ain't nobody going to track us that far, not even 'Pache Police."

De Sana said, "I'm not telling you again, Rondo." Rondo glanced at the hand on the pistol butt and moved out of the doorway.

But as he walked through the pines toward the canyon edge, he held the canteen up to his face and shook it a few times. He could hear the whiskey inside sloshing around sounding as if it were still a good one-third full. Rondo smiled and his mind erased the scowling yellow face. Lew De Sana could go take a whistlin' dive at the moon for all he cared.

The girl's fingers were crooked through the handles of the three enamel cups, and she kept her eyes lowered to the table as she set the coffee pot down with her other hand, placing the cups next to it.

"Looks good," Patman said.

She said nothing, but her eyes lifted to him briefly, then darted to the opposite side of the table where Fallis stood and then lowered just as quickly. She had turned her head slightly, enough for Fallis to see the bruise on her cheek bone. A deep blue beneath her eye that spread into a yellowish caste in the soft hollow of her cheek. There was a lifelessness in the dark eyes and perhaps fear. Fallis kept staring at the girl, seeing the utter resignation that showed in her face and was there even in the way she moved her small body. Like a person who has given up and doesn't much care what happens next. He noticed the eyes when her glance wandered to him again, dark and tired, yet with a certain hungriness in their deepness. No, it wasn't fear.

De Sana picked up the first cup as she filled it and poured a heavy shot from the bottle into it. He set the bottle down and lifted the coffee cup to his mouth. His lips moved, as if tasting, and he said, "It's cold," looking at the girl in a way that didn't need the support of other words. He turned the cup upside down and poured the dark liquid on the floor.

Fallis thought, what a damn fool. Who's he trying to impress? He glanced at Patman, but the ex-corporal was looking at De Sana as if pouring the coffee on the floor was the most normal thing in the world.

As the girl picked up the big coffee pot, her hand shook with the weight and before her other hand could close on the spout, she dropped it back on the table.

"Here, I'll give you a hand," Fallis offered. "That's a big jug."

But just as he took it from the girl's hands, he heard De Sana say, "Leave that pot alone!"

He looked at De Sana in bewilderment. "What? I just want to help her out with the coffeepot."

"She can do her own chores." De Sana's voice was unhurried. "Just put it down."

Dave Fallis felt heat rise up over his face. When he was angry, he always wondered if it showed. And sometimes, as, for instance, now, he didn't care. His heart started going faster with the rise of the heat that tingled the hair on the back of his head and made the words come to his mouth. And he had to spit the words out hard because it would make him feel better.

"Who the hell are you talking to? Do I look like somebody you can give orders to?" Fallis stopped but kept on looking at the thin, sallow face, wishing he could think of something good to say while the anger was up.

Patman moved closer to the younger man. "Slow down, Dave," he said with a laugh that sounded forced. "A man's got a right to run things like he wants in his own house."

De Sana's eyes moved from one to the other, then back to the girl and said, "What are you waiting for?" He kept his eyes on her until she passed through the doorway. Then he said, "Mister, you better have a talk with your boy."

Fallis heard Patman say, "That's just his Irish, Lew. You know, young and gets hot easy." He stared at the old cavalry-man—not really old, but twice his own age—and tried to see through the sad face with the drooping mustache because he knew that wasn't Virg Patman talking, calling him by his first name as if they were old friends. What was the matter with Virg? He felt the anger draining and in its place was bewilderment. It made him feel uneasy and kind of foolish standing there, with his big hands planted on the table, trying to stare down the skeletal-looking gunman who looked at him as if he were a kid and would be just wasting his time talking. It made him madder, but the things he wanted to say sounded too loudmouth in his mind. The words seemed blustering, hot air, compared to the cold, slow-spoken words of De Sana.

Now De Sana said, "I don't care what his nationality is. But I think you better tell him the facts of life."

Fallis felt the heat again, but Patman broke in with his laugh before he could say anything.

"Hell, Lew," Patman said. "Let's get back to what we come for. Nobody meant any harm."

De Sana fingered the dark shadow of his mustache thoughtfully, and finally said, hurriedly, "Yeah. All right." Then he added, "Now that you're here, you might as well stay the night and leave in the morning. If you have any stores with you, break them out. This isn't any street mission. And remember, first light you leave."

Later, during the meal, he spoke little, occasionally answering Patman in monosyllables. He never spoke directly to Fallis and only answered Patman when he had to. Finally he pushed from the table before he had finished. He rolled a cigarette moving toward the door. "I'm going out to relieve Rondo," he said. "Don't wander off."

Fallis watched him walk across the clearing and when the figure disappeared into the pines he turned abruptly to Patman sitting next to him.

"What's the matter with you, Virg?"

Patman put his hand up. "Now just slow it down. You're too damn jumpy."

"Jumpy? Honest to God, Virg, you never sucked up to the first sergeant like you did to that little rooster. Back in the pass you read him out when he started jumping to conclusions. Now you're buttering up like you were scared to death."

"Wait a minute." Patman passed his fingers through his thinning hair, his elbow on the table. He looked very tired and his long face seemed to sag loosely in sadness. "If you're going to play brave, you got to pick the right time, else your bravery don't mean a damn thing. These hills are full of heroes, and nobody even knows where to plant the flowers over them. Then you come across a man fresh out of Yuma—out the hard way, too—," he added, "a man who probably shoots holes in his shadow every night and can't trust anybody because it might mean going back to an adobe cell block. He got sent there in the first place because he shot an Indian agent in a holdup. He didn't kill him, but don't think he couldn't have—and don't think he hasn't killed before."

Patman exhaled and drew tobacco from his pocket. "You run into a man like that, a man who counts his breaths like you count your blessings, and you pick a fight because you don't like the way he treats his woman."

"A man can't get his toes stepped on and just smile," Fallis said testily.

Patman blew smoke out wearily. "Maybe your hitch in the army was kind of a sheltered life. Brass bands and not having to think. Trailing a dust cloud that used to be Apaches isn't facing Lew De Sana across a three-foot table. I think you were lucky."

Fallis picked up his hat and walked toward the door. "We'll see," he answered.

"Wait a minute, Dave." Fallis turned in the doorway.

"Sometimes you got to pick the lesser of evils," the older

man said. "Like choosing between a sore toe or lead in your belly. Remember, Dave, he's a man with a price on his head. He's spooky. And remember this. A little while ago he could have shot both of your eyes out while he was drinking his coffee."

Patience wasn't something Dave Fallis came by naturally. Standing idle ate at his nerves and made him move restlessly like a penned animal. The army hitch had grated on him this way. Petty routines and idleness. Idleness in the barracks and idleness even in the dust-smothering parade during the hours of drill. Routine that became so much a part of you it ceased being mentally directed.

The cavalry had a remedy for the restless feeling. Four-day patrols. Four-day patrols that sometimes stretched to twenty and by it brought the ailment back with the remedy. For a saddle is a poor place for boredom, and twelve hours in it will bring the boredom back quicker than anything else, especially when the land is flat and vacant, silent but for a monotonous clop, blazing in its silence and carrying only dust and a sweat smell that clung sourly to you in the daytime and chilled you at night. Dave Fallis complained because nothing happened—because there was never any action. He was told he didn't know how lucky he was. That he didn't know what he was talking about because he was just a kid. And nothing made him madder. Damn a man who's so ignorant he holds age against you!

Now he stood in the doorway and looked out across the clearing. He leaned against the door jamb, hooking his thumbs in his belt, and let his body go loose. The sun was there in front of him over the trees, casting a soft spread of light on the dark hillsides in the distance. Now it was a sun that you could look at without squinting or pulling down your hat brim. A sun that would be gone in less than an hour.

He saw the girl appear and move toward the lean-to at the side of the hut. She walked slowly, listlessly.

Fallis left the doorway and idled along the front of the hut after she had passed and entered the shelter. And when he ducked his head slightly and entered the low-roofed shed, the girl was busy scooping venison stew from the pot and dishing it onto one of the tin plates.

She turned quickly at the sound of his step and almost brushed him as she turned, stopping, her mouth slightly open, her face lower than his, but not a foot separating them.

He was grinning when she turned, but the smile left his face as she continued to stare up at him, her mouth still parted slightly and warm looking, complementing the delicately soft lines of nose and cheek bones. The bruise was not so noticeable now, in the shadows, but its presence gave her face a look of sadness, yet adding lustre to the deep brown eyes that stared without blinking.

His hands came up to grip her shoulders, pulling gently as he lowered his face to hers. She yielded against the slight pressure of his hands, drawing closer, and he saw her eyes close as her face tilted back, but as he closed his eyes he felt her shoulders jerk suddenly from his grip and in front of his face now was the smooth blackness of her hair hanging straight about her shoulders.

"Why did you do that?" Her voice was low, and with her back to him, barely audible.

Fallis said, "I haven't done anything yet," and tried to make his voice sound light. The girl made no answer, but remained still, with her shoulder close to him.

"I'm sorry," he said. "Are you married to him?"

Her head shook from side to side in two short motions, but no sound came from her. He turned her gently, his hands again on her shoulders, and as she turned she lowered her head so he could not see her face. But he crooked a finger beneath her chin and raised it slowly to his. His hand moved from her slender chin to gently touch the bruised cheekbone.

"Why don't you leave him?" He half whispered the words.

For a moment she remained silent and lowered her eyes from his face. Finally she said, "I would have no place to go." Her voice bore the hint of an accent.

"What's worse than living with him and getting beat like an animal?"

"He is good to me—most of the time. He is tired and nervous and doesn't know what he is doing. I remember him when he was younger and would visit my father. He smiled often and was good to us." Her words flowed faster now, as if she was anxious to speak, voluntarily lifting her face to look into his with a pleading in her dark eyes that seemed to say, "Please believe what I say and tell me that I am right."

"My father," she went on, "worked a small farm near Nogales which I remember as far back as I am able. He worked hard but he was not a very good farmer, and I always had the feeling that papa was sorry he had married and settled there. You see, my mother was Mexican," and she lowered her eyes as if in apology.

"One day this man rode up and asked if he may buy coffee. We had none, but he stayed and talked long with papa and they seemed to get along very well. After that he came often, maybe two, three times a month and always he brought us presents and sometimes even money, which my papa took and I thought was very bad of him, even though I was only a little girl. Soon after that my mother died of sickness, and my papa took me to Tucson to live. And from that time he began going away for weeks at a time with this man and when he returned he would have money and he would be very drunk. When he would go, I prayed to the Mother of God at night because I knew what he was doing.

"Finally, he went away and did not return." Her voice carried a note of despair. "And my prayers changed to ones for the repose of his soul."

Fallis said, "I'm sorry," awkwardly, but the girl went on as if he had not spoken.

"A few months later the man returned and treated me

differently." Her face colored slightly. "He treated me older. He was kind and told me he would come back soon and take me away from Tucson to a beautiful place I would love. . . . But it was almost two years after this that the man called Rondo came to me at night and took me to the man. I had almost forgotten him. He was waiting outside of town with horses and made me go with them. I did not know him he had changed so—his face, and even his voice. We have been here for almost two weeks, and only a few days ago I learned where he had been for the two years."

Suddenly, she pressed her face into his chest and began to cry silently, convulsively.

Fallis's arms circled the thinness of her shoulders to press her hard against his chest. He mumbled, "Don't cry," into her hair and closed his eyes hard to think of something he could say. Feeling her body shaking against his own, he could see only a smiling, dark-haired little girl looking with awe at the carefree, generous American riding into the yard with a warbag full of presents. And then the little girl standing there was no longer smiling, her cheekbone was black and blue and she carried a half-gallon coffee pot in her hands. And the carefree American became a sallow death's-head that she called only "the man."

With her face buried against his chest, she was speaking. At first he could not make out her words, incoherent with the crying, then he realized that she was repeating, "I do not like him," over and over, "I do not like him." He thought, how can she use such simple words? He lifted her head, her eyes closed, and pressed his mouth against the lips that finally stopped saying, "I do not like him."

She pushed away from him lingeringly, her face flushed, and surprised the grin from his face when she said, "Now I must get wood for in the morning."

The grin returned as he looked down at her childlike face, now so serious. He lifted the hand-ax from the wood box, and they walked across the clearing very close together.

Virgil Patman stood in the doorway and watched them dissolve into the darkness of the pines.

Well, what are you going to do? Maybe a man's not better off minding his own business. The boy looks like he's doing pretty well not minding his. But damn, he thought, he's sure making it tough! He stared out at the cold, still light of early evening and heard the voice in his mind again. You've given him a lot of advice, but you've never really done anything for him. He's a good boy. Deserves a break. It's his own damn business how quick he falls for a girl. Why don't you try and give him a hand?

Patman exhaled wearily and turned back into the hut. He lifted De Sana's handgun from the holster on the wall and pushed it into the waist of his pants. From the cupboard he took the boxes of cartridges, loading one arm, and then picked up a Winchester leaning in the front corner that he had not noticed there before. He passed around the cooking lean-to to the back of the hut and entered the pines that pushed in close there. In a few minutes he was back inside the cabin, brushing sand from his hands. Not much, he thought, but maybe it'll help some. Before he sat down and poured himself a drink, he drew his pistol and placed it on the table near his hand.

Two Cents knew patience. It was as natural to him as breathing. He could not help smiling as he watched the white man, not a hundred feet away and just above him on the opposite slope, pull his head up high over the rim of the rocks in front of him, concentrating his attention off below where the trail broke into the pass. Rondo watched the pass, like De Sana had told him, and if his eyes wandered over the opposite canyon wall, it was only when he dragged them back to his own niche, and then it was only a fleeting glance at almost vertical smooth rock and brush.

Two Cents waited and watched, studying this white man who exposed himself so in hiding. Perhaps the man is a lure, he thought, to take us off guard. His lips straightened into a tight line, erasing the smile. He watched the man's head turn to the trees above him. Then the head turned back and he lifted the big canteen to his mouth. Two Cents had counted, and it was the sixth time the man had done so in less than a half hour. His thirst must be that of fire.

He felt a hand on his ankle and began to ease his body away from the rim that was here thick with tangled brush. He backed away cautiously so that the loose gravel would not even know he was there, and nodded his head once to Vea Oiga who crept past him to where he had lain.

A dozen or so yards back, where the ground sloped from the rim, he stood erect and looked back at Vea Oiga. Even at this short distance he could barely make out the crouched figure.

He lifted the shell belt over his head and then removed the faded blue jacket carefully, smoothing the bare sleeves before folding it next to Vea Oiga's on the ground. If he performed bravely, he thought, perhaps Cima Quaine will put a gold mark on the sleeves. He noticed Vea Oiga had folded his jacket so the three gold stripes were on top. Perhaps not three all at once, for it had taken Vea Oiga years to acquire them, but just one. How fine that would look! Surely Cima Quaine must recognize their ability in discovering this man in the pass.

Less than an hour before, they had followed the trail up to the point where it twisted into the pass, but there they stopped and back-trailed to a gradual rock fall that lead up to the top of the canyon. They had tied up there and climbed on foot to the canyon rim that looked across to the other slope. They had done this naturally, without a second thought, because it was their business, and because if they were laying an ambush they would have picked this place where the pass narrowed and it was a hundred feet back to shelter. A few minutes after creeping to the rim, Rondo had appeared with a clatter of gravel, standing, exposing himself fully.

Vea Oiga had whispered to him what they would do after

studying the white man for some time. Then he had dropped back to prepare himself. With Cima Quaine and the rest of the Coyotero Apache scouts less than an hour behind, they would just have time to get ready and go about the ticklish job of disposing of the lookout. Two Cents hoped that the chief scout would hurry up and be there to see him climb up to take the guard. He glanced at his castoff cavalry jacket again and pictured the gold chevron on the sleeve; it was as bright and impressive as Vea Oiga's sergeant stripes.

Now he looked at the curled toes of his moccasins as he unfastened the ties below his knees and rolled the legging part of his pants high above his knees and secured them again. He tightened the string of his breechclout, then spit on his hands a half dozen times rubbing the saliva over his arms and the upper part of his body until his dull brown coloring glistened with the wetness. When he had moistened every part of skin showing, he sank to the ground and rolled in the dust, rubbing his arms and face with the sand that clung to the wet skin.

He raised himself to his knees and knelt motionless like a rock or a stump, his body the color of everything around him, and now, just as still and unreal in his concentration.

Slowly his arms lifted to the dulling sky and his thoughts went to U-sen. He petitioned the god that he might perform bravely in what was to come, and if it were the will of U-sen that he was to die this day, would the god mind if it came about before the sun set? To be killed at night was to wander in eternal darkness, and nothing that he imagined could be worse, especially coming at the hands of a white man whom even the other white men despised.

When Two Cents had disappeared down through the rocks, Vea Oiga moved back from the rim until he was sure he could not be seen. Then he ran in a crouch, weaving through the mesquite and boulders, until he found another place along the rim that was dense with brush clumps. From here,

Rondo's head and rifle barrel were still visible, but now he could also see, down to the right, the opening where the trail cut into the pass. He lay motionless, watching the white man until finally the low, wailing call lifted from down canyon. At that moment he watched Rondo more intently and saw the man's head lift suddenly to look in the direction from which the sound had come; but after only a few seconds the head dropped again, relaxed. Vea Oiga smiled. Now it was his turn.

The figure across the canyon was still for a longer time than usual, but finally the scout saw the head move slowly, looking behind and above to the pines. Vea Oiga rolled to his side and cupped his hands over his mouth. When he saw the canteen come up even with the man's face, he whistled into his cupped hands, the sound coming out in a moan and floating in the air as if coming from nowhere. He rolled again in time to see Two Cents dart from the trail opening across the pass to the opposite slope. He lay motionless at the base for a few minutes. Then as he watched, the figure slowly began to inch his way up-canyon.

By the time the sergeant of scouts had made his way around to where trail met pass, Two Cents was far up the canyon. Vea Oiga clung tight to the rock wall and inched his face past the angle that would show him the pass. He saw the movement. A hump that was part of the ground seemed to edge along a few feet and then stop. And soon he watched this moving piece of earth glide directly under the white man's position and dissolve into the hollow that ran up the slanting wall just past the yellowness of the patch of prickly pear. And above the yellow bloom the rifle could no longer be seen. A splash of crimson spreading in the sky behind the pines was all that was left of the sun.

Vea Oiga turned quickly and ran back up-trail. He stopped on a rise and looked out over the open country, patched and cut with hills in the distance. His gaze crawled out slowly, sweeping on a small arc, and then stopped. There! Yes, he was sure. Maybe they were three miles away, but no more, which meant Cima Quaine would be there in fifteen to twenty minutes. Vea Oiga did not have time to wait for the scouting party. He ran back to the mouth of the pass and there, at the side of the trail, piled three stones one on the other. With his knife he scratched marks on the top stone and at the base of the bottom one, then hurried to the outcropping of rock from which he had watched the progress of his companion. And just as his gaze inched past the rock, he saw the movement behind and above the white man's position, as if part of the ground was sliding down on him.

Vea Oiga moved like a shadow at that moment across the openness of the pass. The shadow moved quickly up the face of the slope and soon was lost among rock and the darkness of the pines that straggled down the slope.

Crossing the clear patch of sand, Lew De Sana didn't like the feeling that had come over him. Not something new, just an intensifying of the nervousness that had spread through his body since the arrival of the two men. As if every part of his body was aware of something imminent, but would not tell his mind about it. As he thought about it, he realized that, no, it was not something that had been born with the arrival of the two men. It had been inside of him every day of the two years at Yuma, gaining strength the night Rondo aided him in his escape. And it had been a clawing part of his stomach the night north of Tucson when they had picked up the girl.

He didn't understand the feeling. That's what worried him. The nervousness would come and then go away, but when it returned, he would find that it had grown, and when it went away there was always a part of him that had vanished with it. A part of him that he used to rely on.

One thing, he was honest with himself in his introspection. And undoubtedly it was this honesty that made him see himself clearly enough to be frightened, but still with a certain haze that would not allow him to understand. He remembered his reputation. Cold nerve and a swivel-type gun holster that he knew how to use. In the days before Yuma, sometimes reputation had been enough. And, more often, he had hoped that it would be enough, for he wasn't fool enough to believe completely in his own reputation. But every once in a while he was called on to back up his reputation, and sometimes this had been hard.

Now he wasn't sure. Men can forget in two years. They can forget a great deal, and De Sana worried if he would have to prove himself all over again. It had come to him lately that if this were true, he would never survive, even though he knew he was still good with a gun and could face any situation if he had to. There was this tiredness inside of him now. It clashed with the nervous tension of a hunted man and left him confused and in a desperate sort of helplessness.

Moving through the pines, thoughts ran through his mind, one on top of the other so that none of them made sense. He closed his eyes tightly for a moment, passing his hand over his face and rubbing his forehead as if the gesture would make the racing in his mind stop. He felt the short hair hanging on his forehead, and as his hand lowered, the gauntness of his cheeks and the stubble of his new mustache. He saw the cell block at Yuma and swore in his breath.

His boots made a muffled, scraping sound moving over the sand and pine needles and, as if becoming aware of the sound for the first time, he slowed his steps and picked his way more carefully through the trees.

The muscles in his legs tightened as he eased his steps on the loose ground. And then he stopped. He stopped dead and the pistol was out in front of him before he realized he had even pulled it. Instinctively his knees bent slightly as he crouched, straining his neck forward he looked through the dimness of the pines, but if there was movement before, it was not there now.

Still, he waited a few minutes to make sure. He let the breath move through his lips in a long sigh and lowered the pistol to his side. He hated himself for his jumpiness. It was the strange tiredness again. He was tired of hiding and drawing when the wind moved the branches of trees. How much can a man take, he wondered. Maybe staying alive wasn't worth it when you had to live this way.

He was about to go ahead when he saw it again. The pistol came up and this time he was sure. Through the branches of the tree in front of him, he saw the movement, a shadow gliding from one clump to the next, perhaps fifty paces up ahead. Now, as he crouched low to the bole of the pine that shielded him, the lines in his face eased. At that moment he felt good because it wasn't jumpiness anymore, and there was another feeling within him that hadn't been there for a long time. He peered through the thick lower branches of the pine and saw the dim shape on the path now moving directly toward him.

He watched the figure stop every few feet, still shadowy in the gloom, then move ahead a little more before stopping to look right and left and even behind. De Sana felt the tightness again in his stomach, not being able to make out what the man was, and suddenly the panic was back. For a split second he imagined one of the shadows that had been haunting him had suddenly become a living thing; and then he made out the half-naked Apache and it was too late to imagine anymore.

He knew there would be a noise when he made his move, but that couldn't be helped. He waited until the Indian was a step past the tree, then he raised up. Coal-black hair flaired suddenly from a shoulder, then a wide-eyed face even with his own and an open mouth that almost cried out before the pistol barrel smashed against the bridge of his nose and forehead.

De Sana cocked his head, straining against the silence, then slowly eased down next to the body of the Indian when no sound reached him. He thought: a body lying motionless always seemed to make it more quiet. Like the deeper silence that seemed to follow gunfire. Probably the silence was just in your head.

He laid his hand on the thin, grimy chest and jerked it back quickly when he felt no movement. Death wasn't something the outlaw was squeamish about, but it surprised him that the blow to the head had killed the Indian. He looked over the half-naked figure calmly and decided there was something there that bothered him. He bent closer in the gloom. No war paint. Not a line. He fumbled at the Indian's holster hurriedly and pulled out the well-kept Colt .44. No reservation-jumping buck owned a gun like that; and even less likely, a Sierra Madre broncho who'd more probably carry a rusted cap and ball at best. He wondered why it hadn't occurred to him right away. Apache police! And that meant Cima Quaine. . . .

He stood up and listened again momentarily before moving ahead quickly through the pines.

He came to the canyon rim and edged along it cautiously, pressing close to the flinty rock, keeping to the deep shadows as much as he could, until he reached the hollow that sloped to the niche that Rondo had dug for himself.

He jumped quickly into the depression that fell away below him and held himself motionless in the darkness of the hollow for almost a minute before edging his gaze over the side and down to the niche a dozen yards below. He saw Rondo sprawled on his back with one booted leg propped on the rock parapet next to the rifle that pointed out over the pass.

There was no hesitating now. He climbed hurriedly, almost frantically, back to the pine grove and ran against the branches that stung his face and made him stumble in his haste. The silence was still there, but now it was heavier, pushing against him to make him run faster and stumble more often in the loose footing of the sand. He didn't care if he made noise. He heard his own forced breathing close and loud and imagined it echoing over the hillside, but now he didn't care because they knew he was here. He knew he was afraid. Things he couldn't see did that to him. He reached the clearing, finally, and darted across the clearing toward the hut.

Virgil Patman pushed the glass away from his hand when he heard the noise outside and wrapped his fingers around the bone handle of the pistol. The light slanting through the open doorway was weak, almost the last of the sun. He waited for the squat figure of Rondo to appear in this dim square of light, and started slightly when suddenly a thin shape appeared. And he sat bolt upright when next De Sana was in the room, clutching the door frame and breathing hard.

Patman watched him curiously and managed to keep the surprise out of his voice when he asked, "Where's Rondo? Thought you relieved him."

De Sana gasped out the word. "Quaine!" and wheeled to the front corner where the rifle had been. He took two steps and stopped dead. Patman watched the thin shoulders stiffen and raised the pistol with his hand still on the table until the barrel was leveled at the outlaw.

"So you led them here after all." His voice was low, almost a mumble, but the hate in the words cut against the stillness of the small room. He looked directly into Patman's face, as if not noticing the pistol leveled at him. "I must be getting old," he said in the same quiet tone.

"You're not going to get a hell of a lot older," Patman answered. "But I'll tell you this. We didn't bring Quaine and his Apaches here. You can believe that or not. I don't much care. Just all of a sudden I don't think you're doing anybody much good by being alive."

De Sana's mouth eased slightly as he smiled. "Why don't you let your boy do his own fighting?" And with the words he looked calmed again, as if he didn't care that a trap was tightening about him. Patman noticed it, because he had seen the panic on his face when he entered. Now he saw this calm returning and wondered if it was just a last-act bravado. It unnerved him a little to see a man so at ease with a gun turned on him and he lifted the pistol a foot off the table to make sure the outlaw had seen it.

"I'm not blind."

"Just making sure, Lew," Patman drawled.

De Sana seemed to relax even more now, and moved his hand to his back pocket, slowly, so the other man wouldn't get the wrong idea. He said, "Mind if I have a smoke?" while he dug the tobacco and paper from his pocket.

Patman shook his head once from side to side, and his eyes squinted at the outlaw, wondering what the hell he was playing for. He looked closely as the man poured tobacco into the creased paper and didn't see any of it shake loose to the floor. The fool's got iron running through him, he thought.

De Sana looked up as he shaped the cigarette. "You didn't answer my question," he said.

"About the boy? He can take care of himself," Patman answered.

"Why isn't he here, then?" De Sana said it in a low voice, but there was a sting to the words.

Patman said, "He's out courting your girlfriend," and smiled, watching the dumbfounded expression freeze on the gunman's face. "You might say I'm giving him a little fatherly hand here," and the smile broadened.

De Sana's thin body had stiffened. Now he breathed long and shrugged his shoulders. "So you're playing the father," he said. Standing half-sideways toward Patman, he pulled the unlit cigarette from his mouth and waved it at the man seated behind the table, "I got to reach for a match, Dad."

"Long as you can do it with your left hand," Patman said. Then added, "Son."

De Sana smiled thinly and drew a match from his side pocket.

Patman watched the arm swing down against the thigh and saw the sudden flame in the dimness as it came back up. And at that split second he knew he had made his mistake.

He saw the other movement, another something swinging up, but it was off away from the sudden flare of the match and in the fraction of the moment it took him to realize what it was, it was too late. There was the explosion, the stab of flame, and the shock against his arm. At the same time he went up from the table and felt the weight of the handgun slipping from his fingers, as another explosion mixed with the smoke of the first and he felt the sledgehammer blow against his side. He went over with the chair and felt the packed-dirt floor slam against his back.

His hands clutched at his side instinctively, feeling the wetness that was there already, then winced in pain and dropped his right arm next to him on the floor. He closed his eyes hard, and when he opened them again he was looking at a pistol barrel, and above it De Sana's drawn face.

Unsmiling, the outlaw said, "I don't think you'da made a very good father." He turned quickly and sprinted out of the hut.

Patman closed his eyes again to see the swirling black that sucked at his brain. For a moment he felt a nausea in his stomach, then numbness seemed to creep over his body. A prickling numbness that was as soothing as the dark void that was spinning inside his head. I'm going to sleep, he thought. But before he did, he remembered hearing a shot come from outside, then another.

Cima Quaine walked over to him when he saw the boy look up quickly. Dave Fallis looked anxiously from Patman's motionless form up to the chief scout who now stood next to him where he knelt.

"I saw his eyes open and close twice!" he whispered excitedly.

The scout hunkered down beside him and wrinkled his buckskin face into a smile. It was an ageless face, cold in its dark, crooked lines and almost cruel, but the smile was plain in the eyes. He was bareheaded, and his dark hair glistened flat on his skull in the lantern light that flickered close behind him on the table.

"You'd have to tie rocks to him and drop him in a well to kill Virgil," he said. "And then you'd never be sure." He glanced at the boy to see the effect of his words and then back to Patman. The eyes were open now, and Patman was grinning at him.

"Don't be too sure," he said weakly. His eyes went to Fallis who looked as if he wanted to say something, but was afraid to let it come out. He smiled back at the boy watching the relief spread over his face and saw him bite at his lower lip. "Did you get him?"

Fallis shook his head, but Quaine said, "Vea Oiga was crawling up to take the horses when De Sana ran into the corral and took one without even waiting to saddle. He shot at him, but didn't get him." He twisted his head and looked up at one of the Apaches standing behind him. "When we get home, you're going to spend your next two month's pay on practice shells."

Vea Oiga dropped his head and looked suddenly ashamed and ridiculous with the vermilion sergeant stripes painted on his naked arms. He shuffled through the doorway without looking up at the girl who stepped inside quickly to let him pass.

She stood near the cupboard not knowing what to do with her hands, watching Dave Fallis. One of the half dozen

Coyotero scouts in the room moved near her idly and she shrank closer to the wall nervously picking at the frayed collar of her dress. She looked about the room wide-eyed for a moment, then stepped around the Apache hurriedly and out through the doorway. She moved toward the lean-to, but held up when she saw the three Apaches inside laughing and picking at the strips of venison that were hanging from the roof to dry.

After a while, Fallis got up stretching the stiffness from his legs and walked to the door. He stood there looking out, but seeing just the darkness.

Cima Quaine bent closer to Patman's drawn face. The ex-trooper's eyes were open, but his face was tight with pain. The hole in his side had started to bleed again. Patman knew it was only a matter of time, but he tried not to show the pain when the contract scout lowered close to him. He heard the scout say, "Your partner's kind of nervous," and for a moment it sounded far away.

Patman answered, "He's young," but knew that didn't explain anything to the other man.

"He's anxious to get on after the man," Quiane went on. "How you feel having an avenging angel?" Then added quickly, "Hell, in another day or two you'll be avenging yourself."

"It's not for me," Patman whispered, and hesitated. "It's for himself, and the girl."

Quaine was surprised, but kept his voice down. "The girl? He hasn't even looked at her since we got here."

"And he won't," Patman said. "Until he gets him." He saw the other man's frown and added, "It's a long story, all about pride and getting your toes stepped on." He grinned to himself at the faint sign of bewilderment on the scout's face. Nobody's going to ask a dying man to talk sense. Besides, it would take too long.

After a silence, Patman whispered, "Let him go, Cima."

"His yen to make war might be good as gold, but my boys

ain't worth a damn after dark. We can pick up the man's sign in the morning and have him before sundown."

"You do what you want tomorrow. Just let him go tonight."

"He wouldn't gain anything," the scout whispered impatiently. "He's got the girl here now to live with long as he wants."

"He's got to live with himself, too." Patman's voice sounded weaker. "And he doesn't take free gifts. He's got a funny kind of pride. If he doesn't go after that man, he'll never look at that girl again."

Cima Quaine finished, "And if he does go after him, he may not get the chance. No, Virg. I better keep him here. He can come along tomorrow if he wants." He turned his head as if that was the end of the argument and looked past the Coyoteros to see the girl standing in the doorway.

She came in hesitantly, dazed about the eyes, as if a strain was sapping at her vitality to make her appear utterly spent. She said, "He's gone," in a voice that was not her own.

Cima Quaine's head swung back to Patman when he heard him say, "Looks like you don't have anything to say about it."

At the first light of dawn, Dave Fallis looked out over the meadow from the edge of timber and was unsure. There was moisture in the air lending a thickness to the gray dawn, but making the boundless stillness seem more empty. Mist will do that, for it isn't something in itself. It goes with lonesomeness and sometimes has a feeling of death. He reined his horse down the slight grade and crossed the gray wave of meadow, angling toward the dim outline of a draw that trailed up the ridge there. It cut deep into the tumbled rock, climbing slowly. After awhile he found himself on a bench and stopped briefly to let his horse rest for a moment. The mist was below him now, clinging thickly to the meadow and following it as it narrowed through the valley ahead. He continued on along the bench that finally ended, forcing him to climb on into switchbacks that shelved the steepness of the ridge. And after two hours of following the ridge crown, he looked down to estimate himself a good eight miles ahead of the main trail that stayed with the meadow. He went down the opposite slope, not so steep here, but still following switchbacks, until he was in level country again and heading for the Escudillas in the distance.

The sun made him hurry. For every hour it climbed in the sky lessened his chances of catching the man before the Coyoteros did. He was going on luck. The Coyoteros would use method. But now he wondered if it was so much luck. Vea Oiga had told him what to do.

He had been leading the horse out of the corral and down through the timber when Vea Oiga grew out of the shadows next to him, also leading a horse. The Indian handed the reins to the boy and held back the mare he had been leading. "It is best you take gelding," he whispered. "The man took stallion. Leave the mare here so there is no chance she will call to her lover."

The Apache stood close to him confidently. "You have one chance, man," he said. "Go to Bebida Wells, straight, without following the trail. The man will go fast for a time, until he learns he is not being followed. But at dawn he will go quick again on the main trail for that way he thinks he will save time. But soon he will tire and will need water. Then he will go to Bebida Wells, for that is the only water within one day of here. When he reaches the well, he will find his horse spent and his legs weary from hanging without stirrups. And there he will rest until he can go on."

He had listened, fascinated, while the Indian read into the future and then heard how he should angle, following the draws and washes to save miles. For a moment he wondered about this Indian who knew him so well in barely more than an hour, how he had anticipated his intent, why he was helping. It had made no sense, but it was a course to follow, something he had not had before. The Apache had told him, "Shoot straight, man. Shoot before he sees you."

And with the boy passing from view into the darkness, Vea Oiga led the mare back to the corral, thinking of the boy and the dying man in the hut. Revenge was something he knew, but it never occurred to him that a woman could be involved. And if the boy failed, then he would get another chance to shoot straight. There was always plenty of time.

The sun was almost straight up, crowding the whole sky with its brassy white light, when he began climbing again. The Escudillas seemed no closer, but now the country had turned wild, and from a rise he could see the wildness tangling and growing in gigantic rock formations as it reached and climbed toward the sawtooth heights of the Escudillas.

He had been angling to come around above the wells, and now, in the heights again, he studied the ravines and draws below him and judged he had overshot by only a mile. On extended patrols out of Thomas they had often hit for Bebida before making the swing-back to the south. It was open country approaching the wells, so he had skirted wide to come in under cover of the wildness and slightly from behind.

A quarter of a mile on he found a narrow draw dense with pines strung out along the walls, the pines growing into each other and bending across to form a tangled arch over the draw. He angled down into its shade and picketed the gelding about halfway in. Then, lifting the Winchester, he passed out of the other end and began threading his way across the rocks.

A yard-wide defile opened up on a ledge that skirted close to the smoothness of boulders, making him edge sideways along the shadows of the towering rocks, until finally the ledge broadened and fell into a ravine that was dense with growth, dotted with pale yucca stalks against the dark green. He ran through the low vegetation in a crouch and stopped to rest at the end of the ravine where once more the ground turned to grotesque rock formations. Not a hundred yards off to the left, down through an opening in the rocks, he made out the still, sand-colored water of a well.

More cautiously now, he edged through the rocks, moving his boots carefully on the flinty ground. And after a dozen yards of this he crept into the narrowness of two boulders that hung close together, pointing the barrel of the Winchester through the aperture toward the pool of muddy water below.

He watched the vicinity of the pool with a grimness now added to his determination; he watched without reflecting on why he was there. He had thought of that all morning: seeing Virg die on the dirt floor. . . . But the outlaw's words had always come up to blot that scene. "I think you better teach him the facts of life." Stepping on his toes while he was supposed to smile back. It embarrassed him because he wanted to be here because of Virg. First Virg and then the girl. He told himself he was doing this because Virg was his friend, and because the girl was helpless and couldn't defend herself and deserved a chance. That's what he told himself.

But that was all in the past, hazy pictures in his mind overshadowed by the business at hand. He knew what he was doing there, if he wasn't sure why. So that when the outlaw's thin shape came into view below him, he was not excited.

He did not see where De Sana had come from, but realized now that he must have been hiding somewhere off to the left. De Sana crouched low behind a scramble of rock and poked his carbine below toward the pool, looking around as if trying to determine if this was the best position overlooking the well. His head turned, and he looked directly at the aperture behind him, where the two boulders met, studying it for a long moment before turning back to look down his carbine barrel at the pool. Dave Fallis levered the barrel of the Winchester down a fraction and the front sight was dead center on De Sana's back.

He wondered why De Sana had taken a carbine from the corral lean-to and not a saddle. Then he thought of Vea Oiga who had fired at him as he fled. And this brought Vea Oiga's words to memory. "Shoot before he sees you."

Past the length of the oiled gun barrel, he saw the Y formed by the suspenders and the faded underwear top, darkened with perspiration. The short-haired skull, thin and hatless. And at the other end, booted long legs, and toes that kicked idly at the gravel.

For a moment he felt sorry for De Sana. Not because the barrel in front of him was trained on his back. He watched the man gaze out over a vastness that would never grow smaller. Straining his eyes for a relentless something that would sooner or later hound him to the ground. And he was all alone. He watched him kick his toes for something to do and wipe the sweat from his forehead with the back of his hand. De Sana perspired like everyone else. That's why he felt sorry for him. He saw a man, like a thousand others he had seen, and he wondered how you killed a man.

The Indian had told him, "Shoot before he sees you." Well, that was just like an Indian.

He moved around from behind the rocks and stood there in plain view with the rifle still pointed below. He felt naked all of a sudden, but brought the rifle up a little and called, "Throw your gun down and turn around!"

And the next second he was firing. He threw the lever and fired again—then a third time. He sat down and ran his hand over the wetness on his forehead, looking at the man who was now sprawled on his back with the carbine across his chest.

He buried the gunman well away from the pool and scattered rocks around so that when he was finished you wouldn't know that a grave was there. He took the outlaw's horse and his guns. That would be enough proof. On the way back he kept thinking of Virg and the girl. He hoped that Virg would still be alive, but knew that was too much to ask. Virg and he had had their good times and that was that. That's how you had to look at things.

He thought of the girl and wondered if she'd think he was rushing things if he asked her to go with him to the Panhandle, after a legal ceremony. . . .

And all the way back, not once did he think of Lew De Sana.

*If you have enjoyed this book and would like to receive
details of other Walker Western titles,
please write to:*

Western Editor
Walker and Company
720 Fifth Avenue
New York, NY 10019